CROSSwind

A Runbook on Praying for Children

John Rajanayakam

WESTBOW
PRESS®
A DIVISION OF THOMAS NELSON
& ZONDERVAN

WestBow Press books may be ordered through booksellers or by contacting:

WestBow Press
A Division of Thomas Nelson & Zondervan
1663 Liberty Drive
Bloomington, IN 47403
www.westbowpress.com
844-714-3454

ISBN: 978-1-6642-5549-4 (sc)
ISBN: 978-1-6642-5551-7 (hc)
ISBN: 978-1-6642-5550-0 (e)

Library of Congress Control Number: 2022901791

Print information available on the last page.

WestBow Press rev. date: 02/28/2022

Dedicated to, above all, the Holy Father, the Holy Son, the Holy Spirit, the Most Holy Triune God, Yahweh, Holy, Infinite, Omnipotent, Omniscient, Self-sufficient, Good, Immutable, Love, Peace, Just, Merciful, Sovereign, Wise, Omnipresent. The Holy One who sanctifies, provides, heals, defends, blesses, counsels, never slumbers or sleeps. The One who loved us so much that He did not hesitate to send His only Son to die on the cross for our salvation.

Holy! Holy! Holy!

Also dedicated to my late mother *(amma)*, Mary Louisa Joy, who led a true life of faith and taught me to pray. My late father *(appa)*, George, who deeply influenced my life in a truly short time. My late father-in-law, Arthur, who despite losing sight in both eyes, continued to be a silent prayer warrior till the end of his life. My mother-in-law, Sarojini, who continues to be my cheerleader and a chairbound evangelist.

My wife, Tina, who is a prayer warrior and who has been so instrumental in the spiritual formation of our daughter, Nandy.

Our beautiful daughter, Nandy, son-in-law Matt, and little Arthur. May God bless and use you to carry His healing power to the world.

CONTENTS

FOREWORD

On a cold January day in 2012, my wife and I stood in a crowded party room of a frozen yogurt shop to celebrate the birthday of a new friend's son. As a pastor, I am often asked to offer a prayer on such occasions. I expected to be that day. What I didn't expect was the prayer that I heard spoken from the mouth and heart of John Rajanayakam.

After thanking our Lord for his nephew, Jeremy, John proceeded to offer a prayer both profound in gratitude for our Lord's gifts and wide ranging in breadth, touching every aspect of this young child's life and the people God placed around him. It was a prayer that could only flow from a heart steeped in Holy Scripture and a love shaped by God's love for his children.

Many of us struggle with the Apostle Paul's call to "pray without ceasing" (1 Thessalonians 5:17). And although the Lord places the responsibility of raising our children in the faith, many parents feel ill-equipped for the task. It is not an easy task but it is a vital one for their sake.

I rejoice that John has taken the time to put into words his practices. This handbook works from the *why* of prayer for children to the *how* thus giving us the tools for this vital task.

The Lord strengthen us as we, in prayer and action, care for all those the Lord has given us.

—Todd Riordan
Pastor, Columbus, Indiana

INTRODUCTION

Thank you for securing a copy of this book. It is my assumption that you have taken it upon yourself to pray for a child who is close to you. Thank you for praying, and may God, the Holy Spirit, continue to support you in your intersession for that child. Earnest, persistent prayer for a single child has the potential to impact an entire generation. Remember God has created a space in history for this very child, and if she or he does not fulfill her or his calling, no one else can.

I am not a qualified theologian, philosopher, apologist, preacher, or even a perfect dad. It has been my intention to keep this book as practical as possible, and that is why I chose to use the word *runbook* in the title. (For those unfamiliar with the term, a runbook is a collection of documented procedures and operations that explain how to run a system.) I am only a praying dad who learned to pray from my mother who taught me that "prayer changes things." I was raised by a wonderful and prayerful mother who was widowed when she was forty and I was six. I had no role model of a father in the home. It was only the prayers of my mother that saw me through some of my most tumultuous teenage years. It was during those years that I accepted the Lord Jesus Christ as my personal Savior.

Years later, when my wife, Christina, and I were blessed with our wonderful baby girl, Nandita, after a few years of praying, tests, and treatments, I was overjoyed and afraid at the same time. Suddenly God had entrusted to me something so beautiful and custom-created by Him. How could I, imperfect as I was, do justice to something as important as raising a child? I did the only thing I knew best to do—pray.

Nandita is now grown up, married, and a mother herself. In all my years of corporate life, during her years of growing up, I never made an organized effort to transfer all that I had learned about godly parenting over the years. Simply stated, this writing is a spiritual knowledge transfer from a dad to a daughter and her husband on praying for their children.

The concepts in this book are not new. As a "runbook," it is a documentation of what happened in my home church in Columbus, Indiana, in 2012. The church embarked on a forty-day journey of focused prayer for the children of the church as well as those we knew outside the church. The process was simple: a wall of prayer was created near the altar and the names of children were written on it. Volunteers took turns praying at the wall, guided by the six C's that were determined to be the most important principles.

The Six C's

✓ commitment
✓ choices
✓ challenges/sufferings
✓ companions
✓ character
✓ calling

As a church body, we prayed for more than 350 children. Some mothers listed the names of their adult children. God performed amazing miracles. Children experienced healing, changed lives, restored relationships, and other significant blessings. I passionately believe that some of the aftereffects of those forty days still reverberate in our church today. Many young people have gone out of the church to serve Christ in different capacities and in different parts of the world. Some of those praying volunteers have passed on, but their prayers linger.

In writing this runbook, I added a seventh C for *country,* as I believe this has become an increasingly critical object of our prayers in recent years.

I have written this book during one of the most uncertain times in the existence of humanity. For the past year, we have been navigating the global pandemic caused by a virus known as the coronavirus or COVID-19. As the time of this writing, almost the entire known world was practicing social distancing (minimum six feet of space between people when in public) and was in a state of lockdown. In a matter of only a few weeks once the coronavirus became officially known, life came to a complete standstill with stadiums, civic centers, theaters, churches, and other venues closed, the stock market and financial systems shut down, and global economy experiencing one of its harshest downturns. Even burying the dead was an issue in most parts of the world.

Fear, anxiety, and panic gripped the world as a pandemic extended its reach with impunity. In the face of the pandemic, prayer was reignited with innumerable groups of people worldwide praying for God's mercy and deliverance. Prayer is the most potent weapon available to any believer. It transcends space, time, and distance, and it never dies. Nothing will move God like earnest prayer prayed through His Son, Jesus Christ, and enabled by the Holy Spirit. Prayers are never to inform or impress the Holy God. On many occasions, they are simply humble cries for help in the face of insurmountable odds. It may be words as plain as "I'm in so much trouble. Please help me, Holy God."

Prayer Markers

It is important that we tell the child who is the subject of our prayers that someone has prayed or is praying specifically for him or her. At the end of every chapter, you can document the requests that were made in prayer for the child. Then, at an opportunity provided by God the Holy Spirit, share them with the child. It will be an adventure in faith building and prayer, both for the person who is praying and the child, when the response from the Holy God to that request is discussed.

The Holy Scriptures in Psalm 40:5 state, "Many, O Lord my God, are the wonders that you have done. Things that you have planned for us no one can recount to you; were I to speak and tell of them, they would be too many to declare."

This exercise will also help the person praying and the child to understand the fulfillment of the promise in Romans 8:28. "And we know that in all things God works for the good of those who love Him."

* * *

I hope you will commit to support your chosen child in prayer as long as possible. The C's I have presented are not organized in any particular sequence. You can choose to read about them in any order. Most importantly, I pray that you will apply them.

May the Holy God give you strength and determination. I also pray that God the Holy Spirit will guide you in this journey.

CHAPTER ONE

Commitment

Praying for Their Relationship with Christ Jesus

The Meeting of a Lifetime

I T WAS A HOT, HUMID EVENING IN CHENNAI, INDIA, WHEN I SAT listening to the story of a young man of a different worldview who had decided to follow Christ. He talked about his journey to becoming a follower of Jesus Christ. As he shared his story, I realized how much he had lost and how costly it was in worldly terms. His newfound faith was not accepted or shared by his family. Everything, including his educational credentials, was taken from him, and he was disowned. Yet he was joyful, his happiness emanating not from his circumstances but from his relationship with Jesus.

Being a Christian is not for the faint of heart, and it can be sustained only by a personal relationship with our Lord Jesus Christ. Every poll triumphantly proclaims how church attendance continues

1

to drop and how people are moving away from established churches. Josh McDowell and David Bellis wrote a powerful and thought-provoking book in 2006 titled *The Last Christian Generation*. It made me sit up and take notice. The authors argued that, unless something was done about the spiritual state of the younger generation, the older generation is likely to become the last Christian generation. The authors, while providing astounding statistics demonstrating young people walking away from their faith, accurately capture the fear of parents and church leaders. "But most admit a fear, deep down, that their kids, having been raised in Christian families and having spent their childhood and teenage years in church, will nonetheless walk away unchanged."[1]

That is the reality. Our children will "walk away unchanged" if they do not have a personal relationship with our Lord Jesus Christ. No pastor, preacher, performer, or professional can make that happen. At best, they can be enablers or catalysts. It is only through the persistent prayer of parents, godparents, sponsors, and mentors that this can be accomplished. If we do not want our children to walk away unaffected by the message and person of our Lord Jesus Christ, then pray we must. No time is too late or too early to pray for a child. From a child's birth—or even at conception—we must start praying for the child. If we do not pray for our children, they stand exposed to the influences of their surroundings, including the most destructive of them.

I was born and raised in a Christian family and went to church as long I can remember, but I never had a personal relationship with our Lord Jesus Christ. I just attended church out of a sense of duty or compulsion. During my teenage years, after I had completed the requirements for my confirmation, I walked away unaffected. From my perspective at that time, church was too boring, and it was nothing more than an ecclesiastical club. It took the persistent prayer of my mother and others to bring me into a personal relationship with our Lord Jesus Christ.

As parents, sponsors, and well-wishers, we desire the very best for our children. If we genuinely believe that a relationship with our Lord Jesus Christ is the best thing that could happen to them, then we should be praying persistently for that meeting to happen.

In John 3, the Holy Scriptures speak about a man named Nicodemus. He was no ordinary person. He was a member of an elite group of seventy-one men in Jewish society called the Sanhedrin. He was very well educated and was one of their most respected members, so much so that even Jesus called him the teacher of Israel. Nicodemus was drawn to request a meeting with our Lord at night. There is speculation that he was afraid of being seen by others. Another reason that has been cited by Bible scholars is that he might have spent most of the daytime studying and interpreting and the only time that was available to him was at night. Nevertheless, he met our Lord, and their dialogue is absolutely fascinating in essence yet mysterious to some extent. As I see it, three things happened.

First, there was a meeting. Nicodemus stood face-to-face with our Lord Jesus Christ. It is obvious that he had heard about Jesus and all the things He had done, but now he was meeting Him for the first time. Meeting our Lord Jesus Christ can never be a hearsay or a secondhand experience. Every child must meet our Lord personally. The connection that He makes when that meeting takes places cannot be replaced or substituted.

Second, a relationship was established. This was a relationship that far outweighed the pressures of people and Nicodemus's position, power, prestige, or possessions. Nothing can sustain an individual during the fog, friction, fear, and uncertainty that the world throws at them other than a relationship with our Lord Jesus Christ.

Third, Nicodemus decided to follow our Lord Jesus Christ and live for Him. When all Christ's followers had abandoned Him, Nicodemus had the courage to go along with Joseph of Arimathea and request the body of our Lord Jesus, ensuring that He was given an honorable burial, which according to scholars, would have been the envy of kings. Rev. Dr. Billy Graham, in the preface to his book *How to Be Born Again*, points out that, in His conversation with

Nicodemus, our Lord described the new birth that an individual can have as both "a possibility and a necessity." Dr. Graham goes on and explains that a new birth in our Lord Jesus Christ is not a do-it-yourself renovation or remodeling job; it is a new birth that only He can give. To quote Dr. Graham, "Man [woman] apart from God is spiritually dead. He needs to be born again. Only by God's grace through faith in Christ can this new birth take place."[2]

Our children will be constantly exposed to various worldviews and philosophies. More than ever before, there is social pressure to accept all worldviews and religions as paths to God. Asserting the exclusive claims of our Lord Jesus Christ will be increasingly countercultural as time goes on. What our children need to realize is that every religion claims to be exclusive at its core. In fact, most of the followers of other religions would be offended at the very suggestion that they are the same as other religions. Like Christianity, other religions have their own disciplines and practices that are unique to their belief system. Following Christ and living for Him involves discipline, determination, and dedication. Millions of individuals are admirers of our Lord, but the number of true followers is much smaller.

As I was writing this book, I wanted to describe what exactly happens when an individual meets our Lord Jesus Christ. In my own way, I wanted to capture the magic and the power of the moment. Finally, it dawned on me that when Christ meets an individual, He is so tuned in to the story of that individual—including all his or her derailed dreams, mistakes, struggles, hurts, and disappointments—that it cannot be captured in a single description. It is our sacred responsibility to pray that this meeting will take place early in a child's life so that the rest of his or her life can be spent following Christ.

Max Lucado, in his book *When God Whispers Your Name*, says, "It seems like God is looking for more ways to get us home than for ways to keep us out. I challenge you to find one soul who came to God seeking grace and did not find it."[3] As a rebellious teenager, I would often come home long after sundown. Although concerned, my mother would turn in for the night and leave the porch light on. Everyone in the neighborhood knew that I was not home if they noticed the porch light lit. God always leaves the light on with our names on it until we come home to a relationship with Him. It should be our prayer that every child sees that light early in life.

I have had the opportunity to talk with several individuals who found the light later in life. Their only lament was "If only I had done this earlier." Their lives had left a trail of destruction, brokenness, and fractured relationships. Their hearts were homeless as they pursued one thing after another, discovering nothing but emptiness and disappointment. Smith Adrian Fedrick captures this in the old gospel song titled "Wasted Years."

> Have you lived without love, a life of tears?
> Have you searched for life's hidden meaning?
> Or is your life filled with long and wasted years?
> Wasted years, wasted years, oh how foolish,
> As you walk on in darkness and in fears.[4]

The early church father Augustine pursued a search for meaning and fulfillment for many years. When finally he came into a relationship with Jesus Christ and became a follower, he said of God, "You have made us for Yourself, and our hearts are restless until they find rest in You."[5]

We need to pray that our children will not waste away their years but early in their lives come into a relationship with Jesus Christ. Of course, one may ask, "Will they completely understand this in their young age?" History is replete with children who came into a relationship with Jesus Christ and then went on to transform the world. Corrie ten Boom was five years of age when she was born again. Our daughter responded to the altar call at the Billy Graham Crusade in Indianapolis when she was eight years of age. In Matthew 19:14, the Holy Scriptures tell us that our Lord did have conversations with children and wanted to spend time with them.

Our Lord took the lunch of a little boy and performed a miracle with the feeding of 5,000 people. The Holy Scriptures vividly capture the story in John 6. My assumption is the boy was alone, and perhaps his mother had packed him his lunch. Nothing fancy: five loaves and two fish. I might also assume that he was a young follower of our Lord. When the time to eat rolled around and a call went out to see what food was available, this boy did not sneak off into a bush to satisfy his hunger but probably put up his hand and handed all that he had to the disciples. What happened next was a miracle.

After moving to the US, I have found it quite fascinating that Western Christians seem to expect that, if you somehow get a person to church, the pastor will initiate a connection between them and Christ. I have been frequently asked how to get a person from a different worldview to church or if I would meet with someone who shares my background and has been invited to church. My experience with the Eastern mindset has been vastly different. The meeting with Christ precedes the coming to church. I have lived and traveled to countries where Christianity was banned and there was no official church. The only churches that were available were the underground ones without any ordained pastors. Yet the spread of the gospel was unstoppable—and fast. Life after life was transformed because of meeting with Christ without a pastor or church in sight. We must pray that our children have this encounter. The Holy Triune God who created our children is perfectly capable of reaching out to them in ways they can understand.

I love the story of Samuel's meeting with God as recorded in 1 Samuel 3:1–9. Like Eli, we need to prepare our children for a meeting with God. We need to have conversations instructing them how to respond. We have all kinds of conversations with our children. I have been fascinated by the commitment of "sports parents"—those who will go to any lengths to make sure their kids succeed in sports. Their focus and determination are admirable. Every parent or godparent has a responsibility to facilitate a meeting with Jesus Christ for their child, and praying can be a start. I heard it said, "God has children but no grandchildren." I heard this explained as the purpose behind the Bible's references to the God of Abraham, the God of Isaac, and the God of Jacob. This illustrates that our relationship with the Holy Trinity is not transferable. Each child will need to have his or her own experience, which may include doing again, doing differently, or undoing something their parents did.

"Man [woman] is a contradiction," said Rev. Dr. Billy Graham. "On one side is hatred, depravity, and sin; on the other hand is kindness, compassion, and love. Man [woman] is a helpless sinner on one hand and has the capacities which would relate to God on the other."[6] One of the cornerstones of a new life is the understanding that we in our own strength do not have the capacity to stay within the safety rails of our faith. These safety rails were created by a Holy God out of immense love for us as well as His desire for our safety and our well-being. These protective hedges are clearly defined in the Holy Scriptures throughout the Old Testament and New Testament. In our attempts to stay within the safety rails, we often rebel and stray away, cross over the boundary, or completely miss the mark. This is what the Holy Scriptures call sin. This is not a reflection of our own goodness or our depravity. Instead, as Paul in his letter to the Romans (v. 3:23) confirms, "For all have sinned and fall short of the glory of God."

My wife and I were driving somewhat anxiously in Tennessee when our daughter had just delivered her son. In our haste and distraction, we ran a red light, and immediately a traffic camera caught our act. For my mistake and breach of the law, there was a consequence: soon the mail carrier delivered a notice of a fine along with a picture to prove the infraction. The document also warned me about the consequences of noncompliance. What if someone had already paid the fine and saved me from the consequence of noncompliance? Paul captures the consequences of our sin in Romans 6:23. "For the wages of sin is death, but the gift of God is eternal life in Christ Jesus our Lord." The consequences of us not abiding by the safety rails that God instituted are shame, regret, self-destruction, and inability to pay the penalty.

Today we are gripped by questions about unfairness, forgiveness, the evil that one person perpetrates against another, suffering, intolerance, and love for our neighbors who don't look like us. It is in the cruel treatment, crucifixion, death, and resurrection of our Lord Jesus Christ that the penalty was paid, and we have the gift of eternal life that surpasses our existence on this earth. This is not done out of vengeance, hate, or a desire to punish but out of the boundless love of a Holy God who sent His Son to be the price and penalty for our sins. Romans 5:8 assures us, "But God demonstrates His own love for us in this: while we were yet sinners, Christ died for us." Finally, there is the invitation proclaimed in Romans 10:13. "For, everyone who calls on the name of the Lord will be saved." The amazing thing about the new life that our Lord offers is that there are no prerequisites. We can come as we are to Him.

As I see it, there are four steps that a person needs to follow to be born again.

1. Admit that we have not stayed within the safety rails established by God (that is, sin) and that we need the help of our Lord Jesus Christ to grant us a new birth.
2. Confess and have remorse for the times we have either not done things that would have kept us within God's safety rails or have done things that willfully moved us outside the safety rails.
3. Believe on the payment that was made on the cross by our Lord Jesus Christ to cover the consequences.
4. Ask our Lord Jesus Christ to take over our lives and lead us.

The Walk of Life

Legend has it that in ancient Greece there was a relay race called the torchlight race. Each of the participants was handed a lighted torch. The race was won not by the fastest participants but by the ones who had their torches burning when they reached the finish line. Christian life is tough and filled with challenges. Many will drop out or pursue other options. We must pray that our children continue to walk with Christ throughout their entire lives and finish well.

Charles Templeton was an evangelist like Billy Graham. In fact, many would say he was more gifted and articulate than Graham. They were contemporaries, and it was believed that Templeton ignited the proclamation of the gospel worldwide. The two men sometimes spoke in meetings together. Eventually Templeton renounced his faith and became an atheist. He returned to his native Canada and went through three marriages. Finally, shortly before he died, he wrote what I would consider one of the saddest books a believer can compose: *Farewell to God.*[7]

It was always my dream to visit the Billy Graham library, and finally I had the opportunity. After we had visited the main library, I walked over to the remarkably simple and nondescript grave of Mrs. Billy Graham. The gravestone simply read, "End of construction— Thank you for your patience." We are always a work in progress till we finish our journey on this earth and go home to spend eternity with Christ. Life will come at us from various directions, sometimes completely knocking us off our feet. Following Christ is not for the faint of heart when one pursues a deep relationship with Him.

The Anchor Must Hold

A very prominent, successful contemporary praise and worship leader of one of the megachurches in Australia announced in 2019 that he was losing his faith. His statement was made on social media. While I cannot comment on the exact circumstances of this individual, I tend to agree with leaders and teachers who argue that the Western church has grown too dependent on professionals, programs, and performers to sustain its relationship with God. Unfortunately, the Eastern church is following suit of late. While the church is constantly on the lookout for improved programs, performers and professionals, the foundation of being a follower of Christ is a deep one-on-one relationship with the Holy Trinity that can stand alone.

When I was visiting Kiev in the Ukraine, I was taken to an underground monastery where the monks lived and died, pursuing lives of isolation and worship. Unfortunately, most of our children will have to live in the real world with all its influences, and we need to pray that they will have a relationship with God that withstands all that life throws at them.

The life of a disciple is structured and, to some extent, regimented. There is an element of discipline in the discipleship. Parents understand discipline very well from a sports perspective. They are more than willing to go to great extent to make sure their children live disciplined, regimented lives to succeed in sports. This must be introduced to children at an early age. By no stretch of the imagination have I presented here a new or exhaustive list, but I suggest in this chapter five pillars of discipleship growth and subsistence. I also wish to point out that we cannot do these things to impress God with our own goodness but only as acts to honor Him and seek a deeper relationship with Him.

I remember listening to the interview of a person who had converted from Christianity to another religion. The individual explained that one of the reasons why he chose to leave Christianity was the lack of structure. Recently a Christian mother was sharing with me that her daughter, who is engaged to be married to a man from a different religion, asked her why Christianity lacks structure. It is my opinion that, while the church today is trying to make worship structureless or as spontaneous as possible, young people are still looking for structure. All symbols, rituals, and customs cannot be discarded or cleansed. Admittedly some of them need to be abandoned, but not all of them.

A case in point: In the days of pre-independent India, in various churches the queen's flag was placed in a particular place on the altar and everyone who passed the flag bowed to it. In independent India, if this practice had continued, people would have been bowing at the altar to an empty space. The key is to be able to explain the significance of a particular religious practice. By the same token, I am not confident that many adults understand the significance of the various prayers that are said in church services. The Holy Scriptures in 2 Kings 2:13 capture the handing over of a symbol. The cloak of Elijah was picked up by Elisha. It is my belief that this was deliberately left behind by Elijah. It was probably a coarse wool garment that was important to Elijah and of profound significance to Elisha as he carried on the work of Elijah.

Not long ago, I was having a conversation with our daughter, who had recently delivered a son. I told her that there was a custom that was followed by my family in India in which, after a baby has been immunized and all the initial doctor's visits are complete, the first outing is traditionally to the church. I explained the significance of that, and she understood why the custom was important to us. In Kiev, I had the privilege of attending a worship service at a Ukrainian Orthodox church. The congregation stood throughout the entire service, and the order of worship was very traditional even to the point of bell ringing, use of incense at different points in the service, and a liturgical style. I looked around and saw a lot of young people. I think no religion in the world other than Christianity has made so many drastic changes to its style and substance of worship to attract and retain worshippers.

It is my viewpoint, that there are six pillars that support one's relationship with Our Lord Jesus Christ.

1. Fellowship with Other Christians

The gathering of disciples is for mutual benefit. Acts 2:42 states, "They devoted themselves to the apostles' teaching and to fellowship, to the breaking of bread and to prayer." This verse suggests that it is an ongoing activity—not a rare occurrence. Fellowship with other followers is an integral part of following Christ. The church by no means is perfect; it is a group of imperfect people who come together to worship a perfect God. We must pray that our children will find a fellowship by which they will be blessed as well as be a blessing.

The Lord's Supper, baptism/dedication, confirmation, and marriage are observances for which a church is needed. My mother always said, "A family begins at the altar." Now more and more couples seek to get married outside the church. Even in those situations, it is my view that the place of the ceremony should be prayed over. My daughter and son-in-law choose to get married in a place outside the church. I prayer walked that place, blessing it and praying that the setting would be sanctified by the blood of Christ. This is important as we have no idea for what purposes such venues may have been used prior to the wedding. There are some great traditions that still can be meaningful at weddings, such as the recitation or chanting of Psalm 128 as the bride and groom take seven steps toward the altar to be blessed.

We must start praying at the time of our children's birth that they will find and belong to a good church or fellowship family. Our children should understand the importance of belonging to a biblical church or fellowship. It is especially important after our children leave home. We must ask them if they have found a church home and even help them in the process if necessary. I make it a point to ask every Christian young person who walks through our door whether they have a church home. We should pray that our children find a church home that is founded on the Holy Scriptures and seeks to honor the Holy God in all that it does. One of the reasons that our children will need to be part of a church or fellowship is that it helps them a proper perspective of the world. In Psalm 73, the psalmist is devastated when his first impression of the world was the wicked were prospering, but then in the subsequent verses of the psalm, he experiences a change in perspective when he visits the sanctuary to worship the Holy God.

There are instances in the Holy Scriptures when God expressed displeasure at the worship of the audience. I have been in churches that had invested in technological changes, painted parts of the interior black, or introduced new concepts in praise and worship among other things, and I have often wondered if the church leaders had spent time praying and examining whether their worship was acceptable to God.

We need to keep in mind and emphasize to our children that we are not doing God a favor by worshiping Him but that He is doing us a favor by giving us an opportunity to do so. Over the years, I have also learned about rushing to judgment on the quality of a sermon. I have come to believe that any sermon prepared with the required due diligence, and with the help of the Holy Spirit, will reach its intended audience. God meets us at our point of need, and it may not be the same for everyone, so when we think that we are not impressed or blessed by a particular sermon, we need to remember that the focus was probably on someone who needed it more than we did that day.

2. Bible Reading

The second pillar is Bible reading. My appa (dad) passed away when I was six years old. Some of the things we did together during those few years still linger in my memory, but one of my strongest recollections of my dad is that every morning when I woke up, I saw my dad reading his Bible with a cup of black coffee.

A beautiful paragraph can be found in the introduction of every Bible produced and distributed by the remarkable Gideons International.

- The Bible contains the mind of God, the state of man, the way of salvation, the doom of sinners, and the happiness of believers.

- Its doctrines are holy, its precepts are binding, its histories are true, and its decisions are immutable.
- Read it to be wise, believe it to be safe, and practice it to be holy.
- It contains light to direct you, food to support you, and comfort to cheer you.
- It is the traveler's map, the pilgrim's staff, the pilot's compass, the soldier's sword, and the Christian's charter.
- Here too heaven is opened and the gates of hell are disclosed.
- Christ is its grand subject, our good is its design, and the glory of God is its end.
- It should fill the memory, rule the heart, and guide the feet.
- Read it slowly, frequently, and prayerfully.
- It is a mine of wealth, a paradise of glory, and a river of pleasure.
- It is given you in life, will be opened at the judgment, and be remembered forever.
- It involves the highest responsibility, rewards the greatest labor, and will condemn all who trifle with its sacred contents.[8]

Bible reading must be encouraged as a daily habit from a Christian's early age. This is the oxygen in the life of a follower of Christ. We must inculcate this habit in the lives of our children and pray that they continue to keep that habit till the very end of their lives. While there are many ways to study the Bible, I prefer the simple approach called SOAP, which can be used by small children as well as adults. This method was originally created by a Hawaiian pastor, and there are organizations that specialize in it.

Children must be taught to pray before they read the Holy Scriptures. Prayer before reading the Holy Bible helps us to focus and see things that one may otherwise miss, regardless of how many times a particular passage has been read. Prayer also takes the help of God, the Holy Spirit. While there are many excellent reading plans, I would lean toward those that are not focused so much on the quantity as on quality, but the key is to encourage children to follow a reading plan and keep checking in to see if they have followed it. It has been my experience that parents who encouraged their children to read the Holy Bible and followed up with them to ensure that it became a habit have always been thanked by their children when they became adults. Have you heard of any parent apologizing to their children for checking to see if they did their school homework? How much more should we be diligent in spiritual disciplines?

Prayer before reading the Holy Scriptures could go something like this:

> Holy God, in the reading of Your Holy Word, open my eyes so that I may see You. Let me hear all that You wish to communicate to me today, and please help me to put aside all thoughts and distractions and focus on Your message for me. In Jesus's name, I pray. Amen.

My interpretation of the SOAP Bible study method is as follows:

- *S is for scripture.* Read the scripture passage slowly, reading it twice if necessary. Highlight words that jump out at you.
- *O is for observation.* Ask yourself, "What does the passage tell me about the situation and God's response to that situation?"
- *A is for application.* Ask yourself, "What is the message for me? Is there something I need to do or avoid doing?"
- *P is for prayer.* Pray that God will help you apply the message in your life.

The key is to open with prayer and close with prayer.

In addition to making a habit of reading the Holy Scriptures, children must be encouraged to memorize scripture verses. Every time I was in trouble and in need of comfort, I turned to the verses that I had memorized during my early years. Toward the end of the 1990s, I went to live and work in a country where Christianity was banned. I was warned that Bibles would be confiscated on arrival. I wrote my favorite passages of scripture on a meeting folder and meditated on them. It took me a while to get a hold of a New Testament in that country, and I was asked to leave that behind when I left that country for someone else's use. I always cringe when I see a Bible in a garage sale or thrift store. We must teach our children to respect the Bible.

It has been a practice in some homes to memorize a verse every week. I still think this is a great idea, but it is best if there is a way to recap that verse repeatedly so that it is not forgotten. I am in favor of less rather than more. It is during the fog and confusion of suffering that we usually tend to recall memory verses that provide assurance, hope, and comfort. Again, leaning toward quality rather than quantity, and making sure that children remember, it is my suggestion that the following memorization plan be used.

At the end of this book, I have included a section entitled "Scripture Memorization"—a list of thirty-six passages of comfort, hope, and assurance from the psalms. I have prayed over these verses, asking God to reveal Himself through them in midst of storms and suffering. I suggest memorizing one passage every month. Have the child repeat that passage for an entire month. In month two, add the subsequent passage while helping the child to recall the passage from the previous month as well. Over a three-year period, thirty-six passages should have been meditated on and memorized. After the three years, it is your option to start over with the same verses or choose another set of thirty-six. The key is repetition to ensure that these verses will stay with the children for their entire lives.

There are some passages of the Holy Scriptures that we will return to over and over in our memories or our reading. The scripture passages that I return to repeatedly are psalms 91, 23, 46, 121, 51, 57, and 90 plus Isaiah 43. I am sure you have such go-to or favorite passages. Pass those on to your children. The amazing thing about the Holy Scriptures is no matter how many times you read them, you can get a fresh insight every time. The same passage can also speak to different situations that one is going through at different points in life.

I have often been asked about the introduction of a Bible app to children. While I am not against the use of an app, it hinders the ability of the child to become familiar with the location of the books of the Bible and the sequence of them. The app simply displays the text, and there is no effort on the part of the individual to search for it. When I was just a fresh believer, we used to play a game called sword drill. We all had our printed copies of the Bible, and the leader would call out a book, chapter, and verse number. We had to search for that verse, and whoever found it first got a reward. This enabled us to page through the entire Bible and become familiar with the location of the books. This is a game that families can play as well.

3. Prayer

The third pillar that supports one's relationship with our Lord Jesus Christ is a consistent prayer life. Prayer, in my view, is talking to God and pouring out our hearts to Him. When we pray for a child and teach a child to pray, we are planting a seed for future praying families and generations. The church at large is in desperate need of people who can pray. As someone once said, the church needs people who will take the promises of God in one hand and the needs of the world in the other and stand in the gap interceding. Intercession is a silent and powerful weapon. Children not only need to be taught to pray but need to be prayed over constantly. It is spiritual warfare for the hearts and minds of our children to be focused on God. We need to plead the blood of our Lord over their lives every day.

Prayer is a discipline that needs to be practiced. A child must be trained to pray so much that it becomes their first response even as they pursue other options. Prayer as a reflex takes practice. Prayer revives the heart of the one who is praying. A relationship with God cannot be built in a hurry or lackadaisically. Daniel prayed three times daily (Daniel 6:10), and Jews continue that practice to this day. Paul prayed night and day (1 Thessalonians 3:10).

I was a very rebellious teenager, and there were many arguments with my mother, but the one thing I could not argue against was her prayer life. We went through many difficulties, and some situations seemed almost hopeless. Through it all, I would find my mother on her knees many days and nights. I can testify to the many miracles that happened because of her prayers.

A child is always a child to a parent no matter how old he or she is. To the parents of children who seem to be stumbling from one mistake to another, I want to encourage you. The Holy Scriptures say that all our prayers are accounted for and do not go to waste (Psalm 56:8). Your prayers will be answered. Paul advises us in 1 Thessalonians 5:17 to pray without ceasing. I believe we can apply this advice specially to praying for our children.

During the years that my daughter was growing up, I followed a practice of praying for one aspect of her life every time I passed a particular place. For instance, when I walked from the parking garage to my office, I would pray for her studies. Every day I walked that distance, I was reminded to pray for her education. I called these landmarks "Prayer Markers," and every day, using such markers, I prayed for different aspects of her life. I have always been awestruck at the prayer of Job over his children. In Job 1:5, the Holy Scriptures talk about an anticipatory prayer and offering that Job would make in case his children had sinned against God. While I am fully aware that this occurred prior to Calvary, the cross, and the blood that was shed for us, I do want to make the point that even a person like Job, who was showcased by God to Satan in verse 8 ("Have you considered my servant Job?"), felt the need to pray for his children regularly and fervently.

I am of the view that every follower of Christ needs to be aware of two types of prayers, and this is something we need to be teaching our children as well. The first is our desperate cry for God's help and mercy when we are faced with dire circumstances wherein one cannot even think clearly. At such times, we are faced with such overwhelming fear and anxiety that we are almost in a fog. Many years ago, I listened to a preacher who postulated that the prayer of both Hannah (1 Samuel 1:10–11) and Samson (Judges 16:28), in their simplest form, meant "Lord, please go into action one more time on my behalf." I have prayed this repeatedly many times in my life when I could not find any way to represent my situation to God. This is a prayer that our children can well use. God assures us in Isaiah 65:24, "Before they call, I will answer, while they are still speaking I will hear."

The second type of prayer is applied when one goes into a planned time of prayer. For this, I prefer the ACTS method for individual prayer. Reportedly formed in the 1800s, this is an amazingly effective method of personal prayer that can be taught to our children.

- *A is for adoration.* We praise God for who He is and express words of worship to Him. Worship, as many have said, is an integral part of prayer. We praise the Holy Triune God for all His attributes.
- *C is for confession.* Here we confess all our sins, both of omission and commission.
- *T is for thanksgiving.* At this stage, we thank God for all the things He has done in our lives—those that we can remember and those that we have failed to thank Him for in past prayers.
- *S is for supplication.* In this final step, we bring our needs before God and ask for His intervention.

In praying for children, I have always liked the BLESS method that was suggested by John DeVries in his book *Why Pray?* Building on the healing of the leper by our Lord Jesus Christ in Matthew

8:1–4, DeVries is of the view that the transformational power of our Lord impacted five areas of the man who was healed.[9] In my view, this should be the outline for our daily prayers for our children. I have made some additions to what DeVries outlined, adding education and economic needs.

- bodily needs
- labor and education
- emotions and economic needs
- social relationships
- spiritual life in Christ

4. Fasting

Fasting is a key component of prayer. In fact, the Holy Scriptures mention that our Lord fasted. The gospels of Matthew, Mark, and Luke capture the fasting of our Lord for forty days and forty nights. Luke 4:2 clarifies what He did during that time in greater detail. "Where for forty days He was tempted by the devil. He ate nothing during those days, and at the end of them He was hungry."

Biblical fasting is abstaining from food. It is not a hunger strike, nor is it a way to strongarm the Holy God into answering our prayers. Fasting and praying are meant to go together. Fasting without praying *is* nothing more than a hunger strike. Self-denial is part of discipleship; indulgence is never part of spiritual discipline. The disciples of John the Baptist fasted (Mathew 9:14), as did Anna the prophetess, who never left the temple even at the age of eighty-four but spent time fasting and praying (Luke 2:37).

Those of us who grew up in the East are quite familiar with hunger strikes. According to Wikipedia, "A hunger strike is a method of nonviolent resistance in which participants fast as an act of political protest or to provoke the feelings of guilt in others, usually with the objective to achieve a specific goal, such as a policy change."[10]

During the duration of a fast, I usually pause at periodic intervals and pray for the purpose of the fast. What is abundantly clear is that the Holy Scriptures forbid making a show or statement about our fasting. In Matthew 6:16, our Lord emphasizes that our fast should include no accompanying announcement or display. It should be a quiet exercise between the Holy God and oneself. It is also interesting that our Lord said when you fast and not if you decide to fast.

Before an individual decides to fast, it is important to assess one's health condition to ensure that he or she is physically capable of fasting. If one is not capable of fasting due to a health condition, then it is my understanding that one can abstain from something else and be focused on prayer.

The traditional Jewish fasting period was from sundown on one day to sundown the next day. The duration of the fast can be decided by the individual. It can be a single meal once a week, an entire day once a month, a weekend, twenty-one days such as the fast that Daniel undertook (Daniel 10:2–3), or any duration that an individual feels led by the Holy Spirit to follow. I have always followed a tradition of fasting on Good Friday and a full day of fasting (twenty-four hours) at least once every three months. This is in addition to my weekly fast, which is every Friday. In addition, I also like to fast on the December 31. This is more focused on cleansing and asking the Holy God to step into the new year with me and my loved ones. When I do my quarterly fasts, I prayer walk my house while proclaiming the Holy Blood of our Lord in every room of the house. It is a way of cleansing and sanctifying the house from any evil presence, influence, or involvement.

The Holy Scriptures give us some indication of appropriate circumstances for fasting by individuals or groups; our Lord recommended fasting as part of spiritual warfare in Matthew 17:21. Moses fasted before he received the Ten Commandments written on tablets by God a second time (Exodus 34:28). "Moses was there with the Lord forty days, and forty nights without eating bread or drinking water. And he wrote on the tablets the words of the covenant, the Ten Commandants." The Ten Commandments are focused on two things. The first is our approach to the Holy God, and the second is our approach to our fellow human beings. Anything we feel led to do or not do for the Holy God or any potential relationship impact with fellow human beings could be occasions to fast and pray.

Nehemiah was another prophet who fasted and prayed before leading a new project or taking on a new assignment. In Nehemiah 1:4, he is recorded as stating, "When I heard these things, I sat down and wept. For some days I mourned and fasted and prayed before the God of heaven." It is always a good practice to fast and pray before taking up a new job or a new assignment. Nehemiah was a tough and brilliant leader, yet he found it important to fast and pray before he started the project of rebuilding the wall of Jerusalem.

Sometimes repentance is also accompanied by fasting as portrayed in the book of Jonah, chapter 3. "The Ninevites believed God. They declared a fast, and all of them from the greatest to the least put on sackcloth." This example of fasting also highlights the effectiveness of group fasting. For more than thirty years, my mother led a prayer group of about fifteen to twenty women who met in her house every Thursday. It was not uncommon for that group to fast and pray for the needs of someone in their group or their children. Family or friends who have a passion to intercede can be mobilized in circumstances that could always benefit from additional prayer support.

David fasted when his son was sick. In this case, it was a combination of repentance and asking the Holy God to heal his son. As told in 2 Samuel 12:16, "David pleaded with God for the child. He fasted and went into his house and spent nights lying on the ground." When we fast and pray for healing, we should be praying for every treatment that is being applied in the healing process, the proper diagnosis, doctors, medicines, and every type of equipment that is being used.

It was a summer evening when a couple of us sat with a family in Boston where the man of the house had a debilitating disease and was progressively getting worse. The wife had spent many days fasting and praying. While the progression seemed to have slowed down, in her mind, the healing that she had prayed for had not come. As the evening wore on, she was upset and heartbroken during the conversation, and in her own words, she began narrating how she had changed from the time the diagnosis was made. Slowly it became evident that the Holy God had done two things. The first was to slow the progression of the disease, but even more, she was transformed and strengthened into a person who was immensely capable of serving as the main caregiver to her husband. This was a healing of sorts. The Holy God promises in Exodus 15:26, "I am the God who heals you," Jehovah Rapha. Sometimes God heals the person who is being prayed for, and sometimes He heals and transforms the person who is praying.

Before making a major decision, the early church people fasted and prayed. In Acts 13:2–3, we are told that the early church members received direction while they were fasting and praying. They were directed to set apart Saul and Barnabas for the proclamation of the gospel. "So after they had fasted and prayed, they placed their hands on them and sent them off" (verse 3). In a similar context, Daniel fasted while seeking guidance and interpretation from the Holy God. His finite mind could not fully comprehend in its entirety the word of the prophet Jeremiah, and he sought the Holy God for guidance.

5. Testifying

I teach adult Sunday school, and one of the first things I do after I open the class with prayer is to ask for testimonies. In other words, I ask people to share and encourage others by talking about things that the Holy God has done in their lives. In an Eastern context, I have often had to cut this sharing time short because of the overwhelming enthusiasm to share even the seemingly small things that the Holy God has done for the participants. By contrast, in some Western contexts, there is a much more limited response, and the reason given is usually "nothing unusual happened in my life." Every day and every component of that day is a miracle in our lives. Every time we are at the wheel of our cars and return home, it is a miracle. Every night when we are blessed to sleep in our own bed instead of a hospital bed, it is a miracle. Nothing in our life can be taken for granted, and we must ensure that our children realize that and give thanks for it to the Holy God.

In Psalm 40:5, David writes, "Many, O Lord my God, are the wonders You have done, the things You planned for us. No one can recount to You; were I to speak and tell of them, they would be too many to declare." The habit of thanking the Holy God is a critical part of a relationship with Him. In John 5:15, we read about the healing of the paralytic. This man received healing and then went out and told everyone about it. Paul in his letter to the Ephesians, verse 5:20, advises them to always give "thanks to God the Father for everything, in the name of our Lord Jesus Christ." A grateful Christian is a peaceful Christian. Learning to be grateful starts at home. In conversations, parents and sponsors must be vocal about giving thanks even for seemingly insignificant things, and keep in mind that every time we are thankful, our faith is strengthened.

There is another type of testimony that the Holy Scripture talk about. That is speaking about the good news of our Lord Jesus Christ and how it has impacted our lives. In other words, giving the testimony of our meeting with our Lord Jesus Christ and our resulting transformation. A brilliant example is found in Acts 22:3–16, where Paul testifies about his meeting with our Lord Jesus Christ and the transformation he experienced. In 2 Kings 7, the Holy Scripture recorded the story of four lepers who out of sheer hunger made their way to an enemy camp hoping to find food. Unknown to them, the Holy God had already cleared the camp through miraculous intervention. The surprised lepers found an array of the best food possible. When they had eaten their fill, they ran back to their country and told the people about the food and other articles that were available there. How irresponsible it would be if those of us whose lives have been transformed by our Lord Jesus Christ did not share it with others—people who desperately need it. As someone once said, sharing the gospel is like "one beggar telling another where to find food." In John's gospel, chapter 4, we read about our Lord meeting a woman at Jacob's well. At the end of that life-changing conversation, the woman ran back to her village and said to all who would listen, "Come and see!"

When I was a young follower of our Lord Jesus, I was introduced to a successful cardiologist whose life was saved from drugs and other self-destructive habits by our Lord Jesus Christ. Dr. John made it his mission to share the gospel. Every Tuesday, he would close his thriving practice early and go to a busy marketplace. He would stand in the market amid the crowd of shoppers and share his conversion story standing on top of a vegetable crate. Two people accompanied him. One was a retired musician who played music using a violin bow and a carpenter's saw. The instrument was so interesting and unique that people would gather to hear him play. The doctor's other partner brought a public address system. Dr. John invited me to join him, and for years, I went along to marketplace to share the gospel. The first time I went, Dr. John introduced me to the crowd and stepped down from the vegetable crate. He motioned me to step up and speak. The crowd was waiting for me to speak, but my mouth was dry, and I timidly asked Dr. John what I should say. Without hesitation, he told me, "Tell them your story." I told them about my meeting with the One who changed my life.

After I shared my story, sweating profusely, I gave an invitation and told the people, "He can change your life too." Slowly, hands went up in that crowd, and I still remember leading person after person to meet our Lord Jesus Christ. It is essential that our children have that experience, and we should pray that the Holy God will give them the courage and opportunity to do just that.

6. Giving

Giving to God

Luke's gospel, 21:1–4, records an incident when our Lord was at the temple near the offertory box, or the temple treasury as it was called in those days. He was observing people as they came to the temple and deposited their offerings. Among the crowd, He noticed a widow who came and gave not out of abundance but in her poverty. It is my belief that whenever our Lord spoke or pointed to something, it was of great importance to Him and a "teaching moment" for His followers. The record does not say that she gave begrudgingly or complained in her act of giving. He pointed her out to his disciples and said that in His eyes, she had given more than any of the others who gave out of their abundance. Paul, writing to the Corinthians in 2 Corinthians 9:7, describes giving as not out of compulsion and adds that the Holy God loves a cheerful giver. In fact, my family had a practice that, whenever someone went to work for the first time, their entire first paycheck was given to God. It was explained to me that it was an act of gratitude and trust.

Children must learn to give to God at an early age. Their giving must be from something they themselves receive. I have seen parents stuffing a dollar in the hands of a child just before the offertory. This will not in any way develop the habit or true spirit of giving. Parents and sponsors must guide children to take a portion of what they receive and give to God. I grew up under the teaching and practice of tithing. It is included in the Holy Scriptures, and it is my view that children must be taught to tithe. My interpretation of the tithe is 10 percent of a person's gross income.

Giving to the Poor and Needy

There are instructions throughout the Holy Scriptures on giving to the poor and needy. Proverbs 19:17 states, "He who is generous to the poor lends to the Lord, and He will reward him for what he has done." Reinforcing the thought, Proverbs 22:9 proclaims, "A generous man [woman] will himself be blessed, for he shares his/her food with the poor." Giving to the poor and needy and being generous to them will have to be taught and reenforced at home. I grew up in a very modest home where we usually had just enough to meet our needs; however, my mother practiced unparalleled generosity to the poor and needy. I learned sacrificial giving at an incredibly early age, and it is still one of the cornerstones of my life as a follower of our Lord Jesus Christ.

Giving to Missions and Ministries

There are two types of individuals involved in missions: those who go as missionaries and those who support them. While the Holy God calls certain individuals to serve Him in a full-time capacity, the rest of us need to willingly support them. Paul, in Romans 10:15, asks, "And how can they preach (the gospel) unless they are sent?" We have a responsibility to be senders and supporters of frontline missionaries. Children must be taught about the need to support missionaries and from an early age be encouraged to do so, starting out in a small way. In 2 Corinthians 11, Paul talks about people who had provided support for his own needs and for his mission.

Conclusion and Prayer

Committing their lives to the Lord Jesus Christ is a blessed experience that we must pray our children reach early in life. A life transformed by our Lord Jesus Christ, no matter how degraded or hopeless, is set on a new course. What enriches this experience day by day is a desire to walk with Him till the end of our earthly life. The Holy God has time and time again proved that no life is beyond the reach of His grace and mercy. Prayer is of central importance in facilitating this meeting.

> Holy Father, I pray that _____ will recognize his/her need for help, and accept the transformation offered by our Lord Jesus Christ. I pray that _____ will recognize every opportunity, when provided, to step into a personal relationship with our Lord Jesus Christ. I pray for the clear and persistent work of God the Holy Spirit as _____ accepts the Lord Jesus Christ as his/her personal Lord and Savior and the release provided from the penalty of sin through His death and shedding of blood on the cross. I pray for grace, strength, and earthly and heavenly support for _____ to walk closely with You all the days of his/her life, no matter how difficult. I pray that _____ will be sensitive to the guidance, counsel, and correction of God the Holy Spirit as he/she is transformed into the likeness of our Lord Jesus Christ. I commit _____ into Your care and keeping, praying the blood that was shed for _____ will protect him/her from all acts and influences of the evil one. May _____ grow every day in the knowledge and appreciation of You, the Holy Triune God. I pray this prayer in the name of Your Holy Son and our Lord Jesus Christ. Amen.

Prayer Markers: Commitment

It is important that we tell the child who is the subject of our prayers that someone has prayed or is praying specifically for him or her. At the end of every chapter, you can document the requests that were made in prayer for the child. Then, at an opportunity provided by God the Holy Spirit, share them with the child. It will be an adventure in faith building and prayer, both for the person who is praying and the child, when the response from the Holy God to that request is discussed.

The Holy Scriptures in Psalm 40:5 state, "Many, O Lord my God, are the wonders that you have done. Things that you have planned for us no one can recount to you; were I to speak and tell of them, they would be too many to declare."

This exercise will also help the person praying and the child to understand the fulfillment of the promise in Romans 8:28. "And we know that in all things God works for the good of those who love Him."

On this day [date]	I prayed for

On this day [date]	I prayed for

On this day [date]	I prayed for

CHAPTER TWO

Choices

THE SECOND C DEALS WITH CHOICES. "WHY CHOICES?" ONE may ask. Various internet sources estimate that an adult makes about 35,000 remotely conscious decisions each day. (In contrast, a child makes about 3,000.)[11] This number may sound absurd, but in fact, we make 226.7 decisions each day about food alone, according to researchers Brian Wansink and Jeffery Sobal.[12]

As life progresses, the complexity of decisions we face also increases. Research also indicated that in one's entire lifetime, there will be a substantial number of decisions that an individual will regret. It is also clear that some of the choices made—either good or bad—will linger for a person's entire life. It is not possible to go back and undo the past, but we can learn from it.

Time wasted and damaging lifelong effects are some of the results of bad decisions. Every decision is preceded by a choice, and it is my view that we need to pray that our children will be guided by their values with the Holy Scriptures as their road map. There is no guarantee that they will make the right decision all the time, but their decisions can and should be covered by the blood that was shed for them at Calvary.

In my study of Saul and David, I am convinced that David endeared himself before God not because he was perfect but because during his wrong choices and resulting mistakes, God could reach him. David course corrected and came back to God. While bad choices produce negative consequences, we can recover from them in the context of grace, and we can help others recover too. God can put us back together.

The Holy Scriptures provide amazing assistance in the form of wisdom to help us make decisions. We should pray for this God-given wisdom for our children as they make decisions. Solomon asked for wisdom. As the Bible says in 1 Kings 3:5, 7, 9–12,

> At Gibeon, the Lord appeared to Solomon in a dream by night, and God said, "Ask what I shall give you …" "And now, O Lord my God, you have made your servant king in place of David my father, although I am but a little child. I do not know how to go out or come in … "Give your servant, therefore, an understanding mind to govern your people, that I may discern between good and evil, for who is able to govern this your great people?" It pleased the Lord that Solomon had asked this. And God said to him, "Because you have asked this, and have not asked for yourself long life or riches or the life of your enemies but have asked for yourself understanding to discern what is right, behold, I now do according to your word. Behold, I give you a wise and discerning mind so that none like you has been before you and none like you shall arise after you."

Luke 2:52 states, "And Jesus grew in wisdom and stature, and in favor with God and man." The passage clearly indicates that there is a growth process in wisdom. We need to pray that children will not only be provided wisdom but also that they will continue to grow in wisdom as they grow older.

Also, we learn in Luke 2:40, "And the child [Jesus] grew and became strong; He was filled with wisdom, and the grace of God was on Him." *The Moody Bible Commentary* explains that, apart from the grace and favor of God, our Lord Jesus had an ordinary life. This to me means that He understands the struggles and challenges of every child. He was not transported to a palace like Moses but lived in the dusty streets of Nazareth like any other child.

According to Wikipedia, the word *wisdom* appears 222 times in the Hebrew Bible. *Webster's Unabridged Dictionary* defines wisdom as "knowledge and the capacity to make due use of it." So if we were to adapt this definition in the context of choices, it would read as "Knowledge, and the capacity to make due use of it in the choices of life." Biblical wisdom, according to James 1:5, is something that needs to be requested. Examining the context in which it was stated, James 1:2–4 makes it clear that it was said in relation to the sufferings of a follower of Christ. *The Moody Bible Commentary* states, "In trials, the believer often lacks wisdom or skill for living (v. 5). 'Wisdom' is not primarily knowledge but Godly behavior in difficult situations (cf. 3:15). The solution is to ask God for it."[13]

We need to explain this to our children and encourage them to ask God for wisdom each day of their lives. My daughter works as a mental health counselor focused on children and teens. I have talked to her about praying for God's wisdom before she meets every child who comes to her for help. In addition, I pray daily asking God to provide her wisdom.

Sekor was a good teenage friend of mine. We hung out together and went to youth fellowship together. Sekor had two sisters, and he was his parents' only son. What none of us, including Sekor, knew was that he was adopted. We went on to different universities but kept in touch and met whenever we came home for vacation. His mother dealt with severe mental health issues, and during one of her episodes in the middle of the night, she woke up a sleeping Sekor and told him he was adopted. It affected him in dramatic ways.

Our jobs took us to different cities and put more distance between Sekor and me. To my sorrow, he became a chronic alcoholic and was drawn into a downward spiral, making one bad choice after another. Finally, even before his fiftieth birthday, Sekor died. I often remember Sekor, who was a wonderful human being. I sometimes wonder what could have been done differently in his life, but all that is hindsight. Maybe if only he had made the right choices when faced with some of the most crushing circumstances of his life and asked God for wisdom to deal with them, he might be around today.

While discussing praying for wisdom and covering the choices our children make under the Blood of our Lord Jesus Christ, I have called out seven significant choices for which we need to specifically pray. Of course, by no stretch of the imagination is this an exhaustive list. This is based on my experience along with what I have inferred from others. The situation of every child is unique, so simply take this as a sample and ask God to give you a more precise list.

- when to wait for God, and when to act
- when to make a vow or promise to do something for God, and when not
- when to look at the circumstances, and when to walk by faith
- when to say no rather than yes
- when to walk away from people, and when to continue their association
- when to lead, and when to follow
- what to hold tightly, and what to hold loosely

When to Wait for God, and When to Act

The Holy Scriptures talk about a remarkably interesting incident in 1 Samuel 13:1–15. Saul had recently become king and was faced with his first challenge. The Philistines, who were the Israelites' sworn enemies, had assembled an overwhelming force of both men and fighting equipment. In the face of impossible odds, Saul's men, who were ill-equipped and being led by a new king, began to flee. What is interesting is that God was completely aware of the situation and already had a plan to help this seemingly weak force.

The prophet Samuel had commanded Saul to wait at Gilgal for instruction on the course of action (1 Samuel 10:8). Saul's instructions were clear. He was to wait for Samuel. Samuel was to come and lead in the sacrificial burnt offerings and fellowship offerings. The instructions for the burnt offering are given in Leviticus 1:3–17. A peace (or fellowship) offering in the Old Testament Law is described in Leviticus 7:11–21. There were extremely specific instructions about the sacrifices, and they were for specific purposes. When Samuel did not come at the end of the promised time, Saul went ahead and performed the sacrifices himself. To a modern mind, it may seem that Saul took the initiative as a problem-solver considering the situation that faced him. But in God's resolution for the dire circumstances facing Saul, his role was simply to wait.

In our lives, we always have a choice of doing something or waiting for God to intervene when faced with the fury and ferocity of our personal circumstances. The Holy Scriptures in many instances require absolute nonaction from those who seek God's help, but on the other hand, there are instances when action is required. We need wisdom and persistence to stay the course.

Based on what I have heard from biblical scholars as well as my personal experience, there are three pointers that God provides:

1. There will be clarity from His Word on the course of action He wants us to take.
2. There will be some sort of validation or confirmation that God will provide. This often may be in the form of confirmation from another follower of Christ who may not even be aware of the circumstances with which the individual is faced.

3. Peace will fill our hearts and lives despite the storms raging around us. Whether we act or wait, we will be filled with peace. This our children will need to experience for themselves.

When to Make a Vow or Promise to Do Something for God, and When Not

In Deuteronomy 23:21–23, The Message version reads,

> When you make a vow to GOD, your God, don't put off keeping it; GOD, your God, expects you to keep it and if you don't, you're guilty. But if you don't make a vow in the first place, there's no sin. If you say you're going to do something, do it. Keep the vow you willingly vowed to GOD, your God. You promised it, so do it.

By comparison, Matthew 5:33 in the Life Application Bible reads, "Again you have said to the people long ago, 'Don't break your oath, but keep the oaths you have made to God'."

I find that two different words have been used in these passages: one is *vow,* and the other is *oath.* Jewish scholars point out that they are not one and the same. A vow refers to an object; that is, a person takes a vow to abstain from a thing. An oath is always related to a person. My point is that children must be taught to take seriously anything that they promise to do for God. While making a vow may not be required by the New Testament, if done, children must be taught to take that vow seriously.

There are two such instances described in the Holy Scriptures, one involving Hannah (1 Samuel 1) and the other being about Jephthah (Judges 11). It went well for Hannah but did not go so well for Jephthah. When we examine the vow that Hannah made, we can glean some valuable insights. She took time before she made the vow, she asked for God's help to fulfill it, and she did not procrastinate or delay but fulfilled the vow without hesitation.

Many years ago when I was a teenager, there were at least two pastors who suggested that I go into full-time pastoral ministry. They were convinced that I had the calling to be a pastor, but I was not so sure. After my conversations with them, there were many meetings I attended where young people were invited to commit to full-time ministry. I never did make a vow or walk up during any of those meetings. I simply was not sure, nor did I take the time to consider it seriously. This is exceptionally relevant when our children take an oath to marry someone.

When to Look at Circumstances, and When to Walk by Faith

Our children from time to time will be faced with the choice of either looking at circumstances or facts of the situation or walking completely by faith. When the frightening reality of a situation stares us in the face, the circumstances may be misleading, but it is not possible to entirely ignore the facts or the circumstances. God is the one who orchestrates the circumstances. The key is the emphasis should be more on walking by faith.

When Elijah was at the brook and thinking he was comfortable, the brook dried up (1 Kings 17:7). Then he was instructed by God to travel to Zarephath, about one hundred miles from where he was. The road to Zarephath took him through hostile territory controlled by Jezebel. He was a wanted man, perhaps with a bounty on his head. Bible scholars point out that Zarephath was neither a beach resort nor a vacationer's paradise. It was a hot place where there was probably some sort of smelting plant. Imagine what may have been going through the mind of Elijah as he put one step in front of the other as he walked to Zarephath. First Kings 17:9 plainly tells us that there was a widow who God told to take care of Elijah. Maybe Elijah must have thought that his circumstances would be better than at the brook. When he arrived there, it was a different story. There was a widow, all right, but she was about to have her last meal along with her son and then die of starvation (1 Kings 17:12). Elijah was about to learn some of the biggest lessons of his life.

God orchestrates circumstances, He knows where each of us is, and there are times when we need to pay attention to the circumstances as there may be lessons to learn. But in other situations, we should be walking past the circumstances aided by faith. Only God can help us with these things. We need to pray that our children will be able to make this choice.

When to Say No Rather than Yes

This is probably one of the most critical choices any individual will make in their lives repeatedly. Our children need to be covered in prayer, enabling them to make the right choices. Even one wrong choice—saying yes when they should be saying no—can take them on a downward spiral. Recently one of our friends sent their daughter to a university nearby, and she was amazed at the number of people who were trying to sell drugs to her. It takes only a split second to make the wrong choice and accept that first drug.

Moses had a choice in Hebrews 11:24–25, which reads,

> By faith Moses, when he had grown up, refused to be known as the son of Pharaoh's daughter. He chose to be mistreated along with the people of God rather than to enjoy the pleasures of sin for a short time.

I am sure Moses must have been subjected to multiple attempts to convince him, but he apparently stood his ground. We need to keep in mind that we need to support our children very aggressively in prayer when they have stood up and made a choice to say no. This is spiritual warfare. They will be subject to relentless revisits from the same opportunity with greater intensity than when they first said no. They may lose friends, be relegated to the margins of the group they were part of, or even be completely ostracized.

The flip side of this is knowing when to say yes. Saying yes and no is the basis of our everyday existence. Our children will need the guidance and counsel of God the Holy Spirit in their decisions.

When to Walk Away from People, and When to Continue Their Association

I am not addressing this topic in the context of marriage. My thoughts are more in the context of friendships, associations, and even places where our children spend time. Nonproductive, destructive influences are sometimes exceedingly difficult to walk away from for children and even adults. This is a choice that children will have to make without prolonging the decision.

I would even put addictions in this group. I was channel surfing one day, and as I was flipping through the crime shows, I stopped at a story of interest. It was about a bright young boy who made some wrong friends and began to hang out in a particular place with them. He had all the opportunity in the world to walk away from them when he realized their influence was not good for him. Ultimately, he was killed in a shootout.

We cannot monitor and advise our children all the time. We will have to set them loose, and they will be out of sight—maybe even miles away. We must pray that they will not be held hostage by such associations and that they will confront the daunting prospect of walking away from such connections. We need to pray for clarity and strength to make the right decision, even if they must pay a short-term price. We need to pray they will not lose sight of their dreams and their purpose in life.

When to Lead, and When to Follow

I have for many years mentored emerging managers and even high-performing individuals in both a secular context and a church setting. I am amazed at how many young people fail to understand this, and it becomes a major source of stress in their lives. God may bench us at times, but that may be only in preparation for a bigger assignment that is ahead.

There is a time and a season to do everything—a time to lead and a time to follow. Moses was in the place of prominence and had a position of status. Exodus 2:10 states, "When the child grew older, she [Moses's mother] took him to Pharaoh's daughter and he became her son." Moses grew up in the palace, and it is only reasonable to assume that he was a leader and person of prominence. But his circumstances changed, and in the same chapter, we find him a shepherd in the wilderness of Midian. In Midian, nobody even knew who Moses was, and he became a shepherd. God seemingly benched him for training. Moses was not only irrelevant but hyper irrelevant.

Life is like a tango. Sometimes we lead, then we follow. Sometimes God takes away from the noise and clatter of our lives to work one-on-one with us. Warren W. Wiersbe, in his book *Life Sentences* discussing the life of Abraham, especially his taking second place to Lot as recorded in Genesis 13:8, argues, "What difference does it make if we must take second place behind someone who isn't fit to lead, as along as Jesus Christ is first in our lives and gets all the glory."[14]

What to Hold Tightly, and What to Hold Loosely

From time to time on the journey of life, we will be entrusted with various things. Some things may only pass through us, and we simply may be stewards taking care of them for a short time. Some things may be given to us so that we may bless and help others. We are just temporary custodians. On the other hand, there will be other things that we need to hold onto, care, feed, and develop. We need to know the difference, and we need to pray that our children will know the difference as well. Of course, it is obvious that we need to hold loosely to at least our possessions, power, prestige, position, and even, in some cases, people.

First Timothy 6:12 instructs us, "Fight the good fight for the true faith. Hold tightly to the eternal life to which God has called you, which you have confessed so well before many witnesses." While I am fully aware that we are merely passing through this world bound for an eternal destination, we need to take seriously what God entrusts to us from time to time. These things must be taken seriously, and we need to know when to hold onto them and when to let them go. The wisdom to make those decisions can be only provided by God. There is a risk of not completing them in case we give up too early.

Conclusion and Prayer

Our children will be making choices in split seconds throughout their lifetimes. Most of their choices may be made when they are no longer under the safety net provided by us. We can only pray that they will approach the Holy God for wisdom in making those choices. Even when they make bad choices, our hope and prayer is that the Holy God will be able to reach them and remediate the consequences of those choices.

> Holy Father, I commit into Your hands all the choices that _____ will be making during his/her entire lifetime. I pray that _____ will seek Your wisdom every day to guide the decisions before him/her, especially in times of confusion, pressure, weakness, fear, or the feeling of being overwhelmed. I pray that _____

will be given patience to wait for You and not to run ahead of You while talking to You and entrusting his/her fears to You. Give _____ the assurance that You have his/her best interests in Your loving heart and have great plans for his/her life. Please provide _____ with the courage to say no to things, influences, and associations that could lead to the destruction of his/her body, mind, and soul. I pray that You will grant wisdom to _____ that he/she would have Christlike priorities in knowing what should be held tightly and what must be held loosely. I pray that even when _____ makes bad choices, God the Holy Spirit will bring quick realization and You will show favor in remediating the consequences of those choices. May _____ see Your work every day of his/her life. I pray this prayer in the name of Your Holy Son and our Lord Jesus Christ. Amen.

Prayer Markers: Choices

On this day [date]	I prayed for

On this day [date]	I prayed for

On this day [date]	I prayed for

CHAPTER THREE

Challenges/Sufferings

LOOKED FOR A DEFINITION TO BEST DESCRIBE WHAT A CHALLENGE is. One classifies a challenge as a variable noun. "A challenge is something new and difficult which requires great effort and determination." *The Merriam-Webster Dictionary* defines *challenge* (noun) as a "stimulating task or problem; anything, as a demanding task, that calls for special effort or dedication."

I have deliberately added the second word, *sufferings*, to *challenges* in titling this chapter. The same dictionary defines *suffering* as "the bearing of pain, inconvenience or loss; pain endured; distress, loss or injury incurred; as, sufferings by pain or sorrow; sufferings by want or by wrongs."[15] Challenges, from my perspective, not unlike sufferings, are obstacles that hinder us from proceeding to the next step.

As our children grow and develop, it is our hope that they will blossom as self-sustaining followers of Jesus Christ and will be able to hold their own. As we release them into the unfriendly, the unknown, the untraveled, the uncharted, the lawless, ruthless world, our hearts sink at the very thought of all the challenges and sufferings they will face.

When our daughter went to college, leaving home for the first time, I still remember how my wife and I drove back home in complete silence. On one side, we were thrilled at her accomplishments. On the other side, we had the sinking feeling about how vulnerable she was. As our children leave home to follow their destiny, they will face suffering, tragedy, loneliness, sickness, loss, fear, anxiety, unfairness, and reason-defying situations. I have read many explanations for evil and suffering from a Christian worldview but have found none that are adequate to capture the plight of an individual who is suffering.

As a teenager, I was a participant at a youth camp conducted by one of India's largest indigenous missionary organizations. Late one night, as we were about to turn in, an announcement was made that two members of a missionary family belonging to that organization had died. The father and eldest son lost their lives on the same day from a virulent disease that was ravaging the area where they were serving as missionaries. I could never understand why this had to happen, and I wrestled with various explanations. Finally, at around 2 a.m., I went to one of the leaders of the organization—a very mature Christian—and asked if he could explain. We talked till the sun came up, and he gave me all the standard answers that I had read and heard before, none of which were adequate.

I was similarly confused and bewildered when I sat next to the parents of a young man who had committed suicide. To contextualize God in our suffering would be an injustice to Him.

I served on the board of elders of my church for some years, and on one occasion, I was asked if I would assist a senior elder in offering communion to a person in hospice. I willingly agreed, although I was least prepared for what I was about to see there.

Lying on the hospice bed was a young mother about twenty-five to thirty years old dying of cancer. Her husband stood by her side, as did her entire family. Oblivious to the gravity of the situation, her toddler son was playing in her room. I felt weak and somehow managed to help in serving the communion. As I returned to my car, I rolled down my windows and stared into the night, trying to make sense of what I had witnessed. The only word that came out of my mouth was "Why?" Then, in a quiet, small whisper came another question that was impressed on my heart. "Can you trust Me even if you cannot understand?" God seemed to be responding to my question with another question. Then it dawned on me that we will never understand or fully comprehend the concept of suffering but that as followers of Jesus Christ, we must trust in His goodness.

It is my view that, even if God sat me down and explained the reason for every instance of suffering that I endured or observed, my finite mind will not be able to grasp its meaning or purpose. As our children travel through life, we will have to pray that they will not negatively adjust their understanding of God as dictated by their suffering.

In the book *Sacred Romance*, authors Brent Curtis and John Eldredge present a concept derived from Psalm 91:3–5. Titled "The Message of the Arrows," they position this in the context that "Christian life is a love affair of the heart" and that "our sufferings work against us in this love affair with God." One cannot deny that the arrows have struck us all, sometimes arriving in a hail of projectiles that blocked out the sun. At other times, the arrows have descended in more subtle flight that only let us know years later we were wounded, when we found the wound festered and broke, they postulate.

The authors continue.

> There were other Arrows over the years that struck in that same deep place … The Arrows flew and all seemed to strike close to the fearful place, a place that said that I was alone in a coldly indifferent world. And even the ones that didn't, I made sure they ended up there. I needed the message to be at least consistent that the world was clearly a fearful place.[16]

The arrows that deeply hurt us are the ones we do not choose. They choose us and cause so much damage and destruction that all we can think of is the degraded past and the doomed future that we are not able to get out from under. That is life.

I am so fascinated by the life of David as portrayed in the psalms. He was as vulnerable as any one of us. He complained about his enemies, all the backstabbing that he experienced, the slandering, the betrayals, and how his adversaries used their words like arrows to orchestrate his destruction (Psalm 64:3–4). As I see it, all the investment, energy, and efforts that we have spent over the years to find a convincing answer to the mystery of suffering has been in vain. Still today, we have no convincing explanation. Maybe God intends it to be that way, our lives each being so unique.

According to Psalm 139, "I praise you because I am fearfully and wonderfully made." If each of us is so fearfully and wonderfully made, not mass-produced, and God is the great weaver of our lives, then how can we interpret the suffering of another individual or even try to provide an explanation for it? It always seems that followers of Christ fit into only one of two categories: those who are coming out of a crisis and the others who are getting ready to go into a crisis. I have yet to come up with a satisfactory explanation for suffering from a Christian worldview, or any worldview for that matter. No matter how you explain suffering to the person going through it, no answer will suffice.

When I was a little boy, sometimes we visited one of my friends at his house. The approach to the house was through a long and narrow passageway that became very dark. It was especially frightening at night. Sometimes we would be playing on the streets without paying attention to the creeping darkness, and we would soon realize that this dark, scary passageway stood between us and the place of safety. So we would stand on the other side of the dark passageway and call out for an adult to come and help us. Usually, it was my friend's dad who responded. He would stand at the other end of the passageway, and as we took frightened steps into the darkness, we would call out to him and be reassured by his response "I am here."

We need to pray that, as our children walk through the dark and scary passages of life, their instant reaction will be to call out to God.

We need to pray that God will reveal Himself to them amid their suffering. I have seen people go through so much of suffering that I have felt sick to my stomach, and before I leave them, they always ask me to pray. I simply pray, "Holy God, we do not understand, but please reveal Yourself to these loved ones in this situation." As the songwriter of the 1960s so aptly said, "Standing somewhere in the shadows, you'll find Jesus."

> When the world is crumbling round you
> and everything goes wrong
> and it seems like there's no use to carry on,
> just remember Jesus loves you
> and cares for His own,
> so trust in Him when hope is almost gone.

I believe children must be exposed to dealing with suffering in the safety and security of their growing-up years rather than being sheltered and protected till they are out of their parents' homes and find themselves clueless to deal with such things.

Blaise Pascal, who lived in the 1600s and who Wikipedia describes as a French mathematician, physicist, inventor, writer, and Christian philosopher, wrote, "It is the heart which perceives God and not the reason. That is what faith is: God perceived by the heart, not by the reason."[17]

It is my view that there are four perceptions that our children need to have during suffering, and we should pray that they will be grounded in those perceptions.

Perception about God amid Suffering

Fully aware that this is a topic that far exceeds my understanding, I turn to the writings of Ravi Zacharias in his book *Jesus among Other Gods*. Zacharias pointed out, "The God of the Bible reveals Himself as the Author of life and as the being in whom all goodness dwells." Building on this, he argued that if God is the author of our lives, then each of our lives is uniquely scripted.[18]

In Psalm 139, the psalmist praised God for himself being fearfully and wonderfully made. Every life has a story that has been authored by the Holy God with great diligence—and with purpose. It is also a story of uniqueness, so unique that there are no reproductions or replicas. The imagery that comes to my mind is one in which, before the conception of every child, God sits down at His desk and painstakingly scripts the life of that child from conception to death, including every single detail, with great love, purpose, and substance. Sometimes it appears we have a perception that somehow God keeps churning out children from some celestial factory with some cosmetic differences much like the features of a car. Even worse, we are sometimes under the illusion that God has outsourced the very act of creating a precious life to the whims and fancies of mere mortals like us who have a hard time remembering where we left our car keys or the TV remote.

When Tina and I had our daughter, Nandy, it was after some years of tests and treatments. Finally, when she was born, I was so awestruck that I was even reluctant to carry her for the first few days, afraid that I would mess up something that God had so beautifully and thoughtfully created. If God is the author of our lives, and in Isaiah 55:8–9 we read that God's thoughts and ways are much different from ours, how can we even attempt to explain the suffering of others let alone our own? In fact, the Isaiah text clearly says, so vast is the difference between our thoughts and God's ways that it is almost like the difference between the earth and the heavens.

What we can be assured of is the all-pervasive goodness and love of God. Explaining this, Zacharias explains, "If there is a story, what is at the heart of it? Not only is God holy, but He also reveals to us the sacred nature of love, to which he beckons us. And from this sacredness of His love must flow all other loves." Our children need to understand that our God is loving, and He does not cause the suffering that any individual goes through. They need to be assured that, no matter the size or gravity of their problem, if it matters to them it matters to God.

I have often referred to Matthew 10:29, where Christ talks about the sparrows being taken care of by God. *The Moody Bible Commentary* explains this as "God's sovereign awareness of their distress, and His care for little things."[19]

During one wintery, snowy day in 2008 when the recession was at its peak, it had just been announced that the project I was working on was canceled owing to lack of funds. I had no plan B, nor did I have access up the organizational food chain to request another assignment. It was a dire situation, and I was worried. The snow was coming down and accumulating on the ground as I looked out the window. Near the heater vent in probably what was the only dry and warm spot was a little sparrow that was as safe and dry as could be. The words of this verse flashed in mind.

During our suffering, God provides what I like to call "hope aids." These are small indicators or signs that God provides, assuring us that He is with us. It can be a verse from the Holy Scriptures, some visible sign, or even little miracles showing signs that the situation is improving or not as bad as it first seemed. Our children need to remember that "hope aids" are the fingerprints of a loving God. Hope aids from God help a believer to persevere in hope during suffering and to have the assurance that God is with us.

We also need to realize that every "normal" day is a miracle and a gift from God. Addressing this in his book *Crazy Love*, Francis Chan wrote,

> But it's easy to think about today as just another day. An average day where you go about life concerned with your to-do list, preoccupied by appointments, focused on family, thinking about your desires and needs. On an average day, we get caught up

in ourselves. On an average day, we don't consider God very much. On the average day, we forget that our life truly is a vapor. But there is nothing normal about today. Just think about everything that must function properly for you to survive. For example, your kidneys ... What about driving down the road at sixty-five miles per hour only six feet away from cars going in the opposite direction at the same speed? Someone would only have to jerk his or her arm and you would be dead. I don't think that's morbid; it is reality.[20]

Our children should learn never to take life for granted. They should realize that every day in which they have the necessities of life is by the hand of God. Sometimes in our eagerness to provide for our children, we fail to highlight the fact that all provision is God's doing and that every day is a miracle. They should realize that every day they have three meals, a roof over their heads, and clothes to wear is a miracle. As in the days of the Bible writings, God is still in the business of doing miracles even today.

God's timing is also amazing. When we look back to past events, we cannot but agree that when God intervened and orchestrated things, the outcome was so much better than when we would have wanted Him to intervene. Ecclesiastes 3:11 assures us that God has made everything beautiful in His time.

One of my favorite poems is called "Footprints in the Sand," penned by Mary Stevenson in 1936.

One night I dreamed I was walking along the beach with the Lord. Many scenes from my life flashed across the sky.

In each scene I noticed footprints in the sand. Sometimes there were two sets of footprints, other times there was one only.

53

This bothered me because I noticed that during the low periods of my life, when I was suffering from anguish, sorrow, or defeat, I could see only one set of footprints, so I said to the Lord,

"You promised me, Lord,

that if I followed you, you would walk with me always. But I have noticed that during the most trying periods of my life there has only been one set of footprints in the sand. Why, when I needed you most, have you not been there for me?"

The Lord replied, "The years when you have seen only one set of footprints, my child, is when I carried you."[21]

Perception about the Problem

Life is not easy, and Christ never said it was going to be easy. We will have to go through pain, muck, and the grime of life to fulfill our life purpose. Sufferings will take us to dark, lonely places and experiences that we cannot understand this side of eternity. Just when things seem to get better, they get worse. David, in 1 Samuel 21:1–8 and 22:6–19, went through one such experience when he was on the run from King Saul. David was being assisted by Ahimelek, a priest, when a guy called Doeg told King Saul about it. This resulted in Ahimelek and eighty-five other priests being put to death.

From David's perspective, just as he was receiving some much-needed relief, someone had to see it and report it to the very person from whom he was running. From Ahimelek's perspective, David's request for help was something that showed up without any warning or time for him to even consider if it was safe to aid David. In life, as someone has said, "the battle chooses us" without any advance warning. A problem shows up that we did not cause, invite, or expect. Satan drops something into our laps. As Chuck Swindoll put it so eloquently in his book on Job, "When bad things happen, they often happen to the wrong person."

Here are some perspectives we should pray our children imbibe:

1. It may change their priorities in life, and they must stay open to it.

Solomon wrote in Ecclesiastics 3:1, "There is a time for everything, and a season for every activity under the heavens." In Psalm 30:5, the psalmist says that weeping may stay for the night but rejoicing comes in the morning. Sometimes we feel that our suffering is final and crippling. When we lose control over the solution, or when we are in a realm where we have no clue what is going on or we are faced with the fragility of human existence, we need to be assured that this too shall pass. But during isolation or confusion, as things degrade into a downward spiral, it may be an opportunity to examine our priorities. Things that seemed so important may not be important anymore, and things that were not important may suddenly become important. Self-assessment may resolve it.

As the hymn writer so aptly put it,
Through all the changing scenes of life,
in trouble and in joy,
the praises of my God shall still
my heart and tongue employ.

2. Small miracles always happen during suffering, and they must be aware of those.

I passionately believe that God not only provides "hope aids" for us, but He is also performing small miracles for us. Let me explain. I was speaking to a lady whose child was admitted to the hospital, and as the child was in a critical condition, she could see the child during some specified hours and be there to feed the child. She was narrating to me how she used to be running late and would pray for a parking spot close to the entrance, and sure enough she would find the sole spot in a packed parking garage close to the entrance. On other instances where it would be raining very heavily, and where she would not have carried any rain protection with her, as soon as she neared the hospital it would stop raining. These are not chance or good luck they are miracles from the hand of a loving God.

3. Every suffering is multifaceted, and they must be prepared for it.

Drawing on 2 Corinthians 4:8–9, Joseph Scheumann argues, "The Bible doesn't whitewash our experience of suffering by saying that it's all of one stripe. Rather, it recognizes the multifaceted ways that suffering can come upon us."[22] In that passage, the apostle Paul wrote, "We are afflicted in every way, but not crushed; perplexed, but not driven to despair; persecuted, but not forsaken; struck down, but not destroyed." Paul listed here several types of suffering: mental, physical, emotional, and spiritual. All of these are different ways that we can suffer, and when suffering comes, often several of these types of suffering are involved. The point is that amid suffering, one should not ignore the impact it can have on various aspects of one's life.

4. The problem that is before them is not new to God, nor is He ill-equipped to deal with it.

As I wrote this around Christmastime, I realized the great amount of agony, pain, and human suffering that Christ experienced. The birth of Christ, contrary to all the commercialization and glitz of today, touched all aspects of human suffering. Take the case of Mary. What fear and anxiety she went through! During her time, she could have been stoned for conceiving a child out of wedlock. Imagine trying to explain to people that this child was conceived through the power of God's Spirit. Then consider Joseph. Some traditions of the church indicate that Joseph was a widower with children from a previous marriage. If this is true, then he was one who had been intimately acquainted with death as well as with raising children as a single parent. The shepherds, according to historians, lived in poverty, and while they provided animals for the temple sacrifice, they were not allowed to enter the temple either completely or in specific portions. The kings who visited were outsiders who may have come from Persia. How could we miss a lying, deceitful politician in Herod, who ruthlessly ended the lives of so many infants to safeguard his own political existence?

Take the case of Elizabeth, who could not conceive. Imagine the shame she must have gone through, the source of which was presumably a health condition that rendered her barren. Compounding her barrenness was the age of both her and her husband. Zacharias was given the honor of serving in the inner chamber for the first time so late in his priestly career. *The Moody Bible Commentary* explains this process very well. There were around 18,000 priests, and no priest was assigned this responsibility twice in his career. It was decided by lots both at sunrise and sunset who would be assigned. Faithfully, Zacharias waited for his turn till he was advanced in age. This would put modern day workplace stagnation to shame.[23] Christ was born into a broken, suffering world.

When our daughter was born, I informed my closest family first. God informed those who were closest to Him: the poor, the broken, the afraid, and those who were dealing with personal tragedy.

Suffering is nothing new to God, and He is best equipped to deal with it. God's intervention may be progressive. Our Lord Jesus Christ said in Matthew 6:34, "Each day has enough trouble of its own." Our challenges and sufferings will not be the only things that demand our energy and our attention. There will be the regular events of life as well. God is mindful of that and may give us just enough to carry us through each day. God may also provide a solution that evolves, meaning He takes us one step at a time. Most of the individuals who did extraordinary things in the Holy Scriptures were given direction gradually, never knowing the full plan. Moses is a classic case in point. When he led the Israelites out of Egypt, God provided him direction one step at a time. Finally, it has been my experience that God sometimes provides an interim solution.

5. Suffering is not random and always has a purpose. They must recognize it by praying *about it*.

There is one thing we can clearly learn from the lives of Moses, Joseph, David, and other people in the Holy Scriptures. Their suffering was to fulfill a larger purpose in their lives. Imagine if these individuals had not recognized that and had been bogged down by their suffering.

The purpose of suffering can be realized only through prayer and a close walk with God. Prayer sees God's purpose in suffering and prays for it. This may seem rather intuitive, but suffering has sent many people in the wrong direction—away from God. Prayer will help us stay in sync with God and avoid being overwhelmed by doubt or unbelief. One must be careful that one is not trying to find answers to or relief from one's suffering but only the purpose behind it. As one discovers purpose, it can help drive some life-altering decisions: discovering one's calling, becoming equipped to deal with others who are going through similar suffering, providing hope in the lives of others, evaluating options to make an impact with the rest of their lives, and finally but most importantly, testifying to the glory of God.

Dr. Mary Verghese graduated from one of the most prestigious medical institutions in India, Christian Medical College Vellore, which was founded by the famous American missionary Dr. Ida

Scudder, who graduated from the Cornell Medical College in 1899. Dr. Verghese wanted to specialize in gynecology and was pursuing her training as a gynecologist. It was during this time she was involved in a car wreck that left her paralyzed from the hips down. She was then introduced to British missionary Dr. Paul Brand, who had done pioneering work in Hansen's disease, also known as leprosy at that time. Dr. Brand suggested to Dr. Verghese that she could operate on the hands of those with Hansen's disease even while sitting in her wheelchair. Dr. Verghese learned a completely new skill and operated on thousands of patients, improving their quality of life. She saw purpose through her suffering.

Perception of Oneself

Well-known gospel singer Wintley Phipps said, "It is in the quiet crucible of your personal, private suffering that your noblest dreams are born, and God's greatest gift given in compensation for what you have been through."

Amid suffering, our children will experience blaming themselves, guilt, regret, and a slew of other emotions. They are likely to go repeatedly in their minds to the circumstances that led to a particular situation. More importantly, in the chaos and confusion of what they are facing, questions about themselves may occur to them. It is my view that this will be one of the most important prayers that a parent, sponsor, or godparent will pray for them. We need to pray that our children will have the will and the mindset to get up and get going, that even in the worst of dire situations it will get better, and that they can get up and swing again, one punch and one move at a time. We must pray that they will become more capable because of the suffering and will be open to what God is going to pour into their lives. We need to pray that they assume responsibility, act, make the tough decisions, and follow through on them. When I read the story of David and Saul, I think the greatest difference between them is that God could reach David during his failure, pain, and suffering. He could not do the same with Saul. We must pray that our children, with God's help, will rise.

There will be a tendency to compare their situation with those of others.

During their suffering and challenges, our children will be tempted to compare their circumstances to those around them. A former US President wisely said, "Comparison is the thief of joy." Comparison belittles our hard work, demeans the unique journey we have taken, paralyzes us emotionally, and drives us to despair and hopelessness. We must pray that our children will stay focused on their own circumstances and resist this tendency.

The Holy Scriptures address comparison in Galatians 6:4–5. "Each one should test his own actions. Then he can take pride in himself, without comparing himself to somebody else, for each one should carry his own load." Expounding on these verses, *The Moody Bible Commentary* explains that the only type of examination that is healthy, according to verse 6:3, is self-evaluation.[24]

I have come from a traditional practice by which something was always given up during the season of Lent and fasting as a discipline was practiced. When I first came to the US, I shared my practice with others in the context of religious disciplines and traditions in India. However, not long after, I met a woman from Korea who fasted for almost the entire forty days of Lent and hardly spoke about it. Comparison not only steals our joy but also ruins relationships, as experts point out. Children need to learn that what seems to be a "perfect life" in others is a mirage and, on closer understanding, can reveal problems and pain of a different sort.

They should trust God amid fear and anxiety.

I have listened to preachers who preach against being fearful during suffering. While this may be true in one sense, fear is addressed at least 365 times in the Holy Scriptures. I do not think that God's expectation is that we should not be fearful but that we should trust Him amid our fear and anxiety.

David writes about this in Psalm 56:3–4. "When I am afraid, I will trust in you. In God whose word I praise, in God I trust; I will not be afraid. What can mortal man do to me?" David, Moses, and others in the Holy Scriptures experienced fear. Therefore, in my view, our children must learn to deal with fear by implicitly trusting in God and depending on Him.

As David mentions in Psalm 57:1, "I will take refuge in the shadow of your wings until the disaster has passed." I believe God takes our fear and anxiety very seriously. In the Sermon on the Mount that begins in Matthew 5 and continues into chapter 6, our Lord Jesus Christ uses the term "worry" or "anxious" six times. He seems to be advising a new attitude and perspective that is reliant on God.

Prayers in times of suffering

Some of us have the feeling that God will somehow hear the prayers of other people who we deem to be holier than we are. This is more prevalent in the Eastern context where people seek out miracle workers, healers, prophets, and such to pray for them. Throughout the Holy Scriptures, we are assured that God will answer our prayers and that we do not need to go through anyone else to get God's attention. In Jeremiah 33:3, God directs us to call on Him directly. "Call to me and I will answer you and tell you great and unsearchable things you do not know." Miracle workers, healers, and prophets will all be gone or compromised at some point in time. Christ, through His death and resurrection, is now seated on the right hand of God interceding for us. Who can beat that either in heaven or on earth? When a suffering individual calls upon the Father, his or her prayer is carefully aided, carried by God the Holy Spirit, and spoken for by God the Son Himself. God will hear our prayers, and our children need to know that they can directly access the Triune God.

Perception on Spiritual Warfare

In my search for a worldly perspective on spiritual warfare, I checked Wikipedia and found the following: "Spiritual warfare is the Christian concept of fighting against the work of preternatural evil forces. It is based on the biblical belief in evil spirits, or demons, that are said to intervene in human affairs in various ways."[25] What needs to be kept in mind is that regardless of denominational leanings, the Holy Scriptures address spiritual warfare extensively, and our Lord Jesus Christ was subject to it Himself.

Paul in Ephesians 6:12 deals with this topic. "For our struggle is not against flesh and blood, but against the authorities, against the powers of this dark world and against the spiritual forces of evil in the heavenly realms."

During my years as an elder of my church, I was part of a group of elders that went to homes of our members to pray over them, especially when they felt that some unusual happenings were occurring in their homes. While it is not my intent to go into the identification of manifestations of satanic activity, I would like to focus on the preventive aspects of spiritual warfare. If a follower of our Lord Jesus Christ is not vigilant, then Satan moves in and occupies their lives. It must be mentioned in this context that Satan is focused on every Christ follower, not just pastors, preachers, evangelists, and missionaries. It is my view that any follower of our Lord Jesus Christ who wants to place Him front and center in their lives will be in the crosshairs of Satan.

I heard a story that, in some sense, explains the satanic occupation and control that takes place. A piano was placed in a particular place in a man's house and was watched over by the owner with great zeal and diligence. The man's neighbor thought that the piano should be facing a different direction and tried to convince him of it. The owner was resilient and refused. The neighbor then started moving the piano one inch at a time every time he visited. Before long, with small seemingly insignificant moves, the piano was moved.

Paul's exhortation also makes clear that we should take Satan's threats seriously when he talks about a structure, hierarchy, and organization in Satan's operations. When our Lord Jesus Christ encountered Satan in the New Testament, Luke 4:1–14, it is evident that there were three broad areas of attack: physical, mental, and spiritual. I believe that this can be mapped broadly to the three areas of growth described in Luke 2:52. "And Jesus grew in wisdom and stature, and in favor with God and men." Also, what must be kept in mind from the Luke 4 passage is that Satan is relentless, always waiting for an "opportune" time to attack. We must pray for a hedge of protection to be erected around our children in those three areas.

In his book *The Bait of Satan*, John Bevere addresses an area of great importance in this context.

> One of his [Satan's] most deceptive and insidious kinds of bait is something every Christian has encountered—offense. Actually offense itself is not deadly—if it stays in the trap. But if we pick it up and consume it and feed on it in our hearts, then we have become offended. Offended people produce much fruit, such as hurt, anger, outrage, jealousy, resentment, strife, bitterness, hatred, and envy. Some of the consequences of picking up an offense are insults, attacks, wounding, division, separation, broken relationships, betrayal and backsliding.[26]

Focusing on preventive maneuvers, it must be emphasized that no preventive action can be mounted without a relationship with God.

Based on my experience, the advice of other Christians, and the Holy Scriptures, following is a list of things that every follower of our Lord Jesus Christ must avoid and to which our children must not be exposed. They must also be warned about these.

- Chuck D. Pierce provides a helpful list in *The Spiritual Warfare Handbook,* postulating that spiritual warfare includes anything that is rooted in the occult, such as
  o psychics
  o astrologers
  o tarot cards
  o Ouija boards
  o astrologers
  o horoscopes
  o clairvoyants
  o mediums
  o witchcraft
  o divination[27]
- False prophets. It has been my experience that true prophecy ministering to an individual happens when the prophet does not ask for any details from the individual. On the other hand, there are so-called prophets who ask for details before they prophesy. The latter is not the kind of prophecy that the Holy Scriptures include.
- Idols and images of gods and goddesses. In this age of global travel, it is not uncommon for other cultures to present graphic images or idols of their own gods and goddesses. It has been my observation that some Christians can be very enthusiastic about receiving them and giving them places of prominence in their homes or offices. Recently one of the churches I visited had on display a huge picture of a Hindu goddess in one of its rooms. The story behind it was that, during one of their mission trips to India, they were given the image as a gift. Not knowing what it was, they hung it on the mission room wall. It has been my experience that people from other religions do not get offended when you ask them the significance or meaning of the gift. It is best to learn of the meaning and significance and then pass it on to someone from

the religion of its origin who will appreciate it. The Holy Scriptures are unmistakably clear about entertaining and giving prominence to gods and goddesses other than the Christian Triune God. In fact, it is addressed in the first three of the Ten Commandments.

- Talismans. Wikipedia defines a talisman as "any object ascribed with religious or magical powers intended to protect, heal or even harm individuals for whom they are made. Talismans are often portable objects carried on someone in a variety of ways, but they can also be installed permanently in architecture."[28]
- Fetishes.
- Any games that involve invoking the spirits or seeking their guidance.
- TV entertainment. By way of abundant caution, even some television shows should be avoided, including reality shows that focus on communicating with spirits.
- Objects. I have known several Christians who are familiar with spiritual warfare to caution that demonic forces could inhabit objects and create havoc in a home. Therefore, it is particularly important that any object purchased or found, including those at flea markets and used goods stores, should be examined to see if they represent foreign gods, false religions, occult objects, or secret society objects.
- Places of residence. Whenever a new home is bought or rented, it must be cleansed by proclaiming the blood of our Lord Jesus Christ over the premises and asking the Holy Triune God to drive out any demonic influence that remains from the previous occupants. Even after occupation, it is important that Christians periodically prayer walk their homes while proclaiming and pleading the blood of our Lord Jesus Christ over every nook and corner. I typically do this after fasting and praying. Children's rooms in particular must be so cleansed.

Having said that our children need to have a perception of spiritual warfare, it is important that we pray that they put on the armor of God constantly. Derek Prince, in his book *Spiritual Warfare*, enumerates the elements of the armor of God as truth and righteousness which, when compared with 1 Thessalonians 5:8, can be understood as faith and love. It is a kind of righteousness that comes not from any dogma, denomination, or "holier than thou" attitude but from faith and love which comes from God.[29] Expanding on this, it appears to me that Paul is talking about an intimate firsthand relationship with God.

A remarkably interesting event is recorded in Acts 19:13–16 when some individuals were engaging in spiritual warfare with disastrous consequences. I had a firsthand experience of this early in my spiritual journey. I was asked to accompany a young man, who was reportedly demon possessed, to see a person who was known to have the gift of casting out demons. I remember that trip very clearly. When the possessed man was prayed over, it was strangely quiet. Then immediately after the prayer, the possessed man stood and began revealing everything about the man who had prayed over him. My point is that we need to have a personal relationship with God and that the warfare is led and executed by God.

The third piece of the armor of God is the shoes of the preparation for the gospel. This piece of armor, according to Prince, deals with the ability to be mobile and march distances with speed. But at the core of this is an understanding of the gospel in its fullness without dilution or accommodation. The shedding of blood, sacrifice, death, and resurrection of our Lord Jesus Christ is at the core of spiritual warfare, and the tip of the spear is the blood that was shed for us on the cross at Calvary. The blood that was shed for us on the cross is the red-hot spot that terrifies Satan. If one does not understand this or believe in this, the battle is lost even before it begins.[30]

The shield of faith in this context, experts say, is a large, rectangular shield used by Roman soldiers of that time, almost like a door. Because of its dimensions, this shield, if used properly, could defend any part of a soldier's body. When we face off against Satan, we need to have a piece of equipment, figuratively, like the shield to protect us. Prince points out that if Satan is not able to get to us directly, he will attack those who are close to us or things that have been entrusted to us. We must have a shield that can protect us and those around us.[31]

Michael Ramsden argues, "Faith is not psychological" but is based on truth and reality. He goes on to point out that biblical faith is a gift but not the gift of stupidity, nor is it wishful thinking or something one believes in despite lack of evidence.[32]

The helmet of salvation is next on the list of protective gear. The helmet, researchers say, is the oldest version of personal protective equipment. It prevents "head injury" among followers of our Lord Jesus Christ. Someone once imagined that Satan held an exhibition of all the tools that he uses to attack followers of our Lord Jesus Christ. On proud display was a small but lethal tool. When asked about it, Satan explained that it was the tool of discouragement. Satan relentlessly attacks our head—that is, our mind—with weapons such as the tool of discouragement, tempting us with offense and doubt. As Prince rightly points out, once we are injured in the head, it becomes exceedingly difficult to use the other pieces of armor effectively.

Prince also makes a remarkably interesting point about Satan's temptation of our Lord Jesus Christ in the wilderness—namely that he used doubt as his primary tool. Satan began every temptation with the word *if.* Every person who has used a helmet will understand that, for the helmet to be effective, the straps must be adjusted correctly and the helmet properly secured to the head. For many years, the town in India in which I grew up did not make wearing a helmet mandatory while bike riding. Finally, it was made mandatory, and the police enforced it. Some riders, to fool the police, would place a helmet on their heads without securing it. While they may have fooled the police, it did not protect them from danger or death caused when there was a crash or a fall. The first thing to fly on impact was the helmet.

I do believe that, once a person accepts our Lord Jesus Christ as their Savior, they are recipients of the salvation that is offered to them. However, we must make sure that our helmet of salvation is secured. Any unconfessed sin or backsliding will need to be confessed and the relationship with the Holy God maintained.

The last offensive—and defensive—weapon is the sword of the Spirit. The Holy Scriptures compare God's Word to a sword in Hebrews 4:12 but only sharper. "For the word of God is living and active. Sharper than any double-edged sword." Our Lord Jesus Christ used this when Satan tempted Him. We will not be able to engage in spiritual warfare if we disregard or belittle the Holy Word of God or its divine authorship. The believer must either accept the Holy Bible in its entirety or none of it at all. We cannot pick and choose verses or passages that are convenient to us. While we may not be able to grasp or fully understand everything in the Holy Scriptures, this does not render it untrue or inauthentic.

Derek Prince postulates that, during the temptations of our Lord Jesus Christ, even Satan did not argue with the authority of the scriptures. Satan knows the scriptures better than most of us, and he will misapply them in an effort to manipulate us if we are not careful to resist him.[33]

In a discussion spiritual warfare, one thing we cannot ignore is the blood of our Lord Jesus Christ that was shed on an altar called Calvary. God loved an errant humanity so much that He sent His only son to die on Calvary as a sacrifice. Our Lord's treatment after the Last Supper, right up to His crucifixion and death, was bloody and horrific.

Dr. Joseph Bergeron, in his book *The Crucifixion of Jesus: A Medical Doctor Examines the Death and Resurrection of Christ*, states,

> The condemned prisoner (crucarius) was placed in the custody of an execution team of Roman soldiers. The executioners were supervised by a centurion. To begin with, the naked victim was tied to a post and scourged over the whole body. A scourging whip,

called flagrum or flagellum, consisted of leather strips with dumbbell shaped pieces of lead tied to the ends of the strips. In Hebrew law, scourging beyond forty lashes was not permitted. Romans had no lash limit. Only the victim should not be beaten to death prior to crucifixion. Multiple soldiers participated in scourging each victim. Scourging and torture prior to crucifixion was grisly and brought the condemned victim close to death. It is easily conceivable that the lashes would cut deeply through the flesh.[34]

The fourth-century church historian Eusebius described scourging practices prior to crucifixion. "Bystanders were struck with amazement when they saw them lacerated with scourges even to the innermost veins and arteries, so that the hidden inward parts of the body, both their bowels and their members, were exposed to view."

We do not take the blood that was shed for us lightly. Derek Prince, in a sermon titled "God's Atomic Weapon: The Blood of Jesus," offers what I believe to be one of the most comprehensive explanations on invoking the blood of Jesus Christ in spiritual warfare. Anchoring his teaching on Revelation 12:11, he says, "They overcame him (Satan) by the blood of the Lamb and by the word of their testimony; they did not love their lives so much as to shrink from death." Prince points out that the three key words are *testify, word* and *blood*. According to him, "We testify personally to what the Word [Holy Scriptures] says the blood does for us." He then goes on to list five declarations or five verses that clearly describe what the blood does for us. Following are the declarations and related verses as suggested by Prince:

- Declaration 1: Ephesians 1:7 states, "In Him we have redemption through His blood, the forgiveness of sins, in accordance with the riches of God's Grace." According to this scripture, through the blood of our Lord Jesus Christ,

I am redeemed out of the clutches of the Devil, and all my sins are forgiven.

- Declaration 2: 1 John 1:7 states, "But if we walk in the light, as He is in the light, we have fellowship with one another, and the blood of Our Lord Jesus Christ His son, purifies us from all sin." According to this scripture, the blood of our Lord Jesus Christ, God's Son, continually cleanses me from all sin.

- Declaration 3: Romans 5:9 states, "Since we have been justified by His blood, how much more shall we be saved from God's wrath through Him." According to this scripture, through the blood of our Lord Jesus Christ I am justified, made righteous, just as if I had never sinned.

- Declaration 4: Hebrews 13:12 states, "And so Jesus also suffered outside the city gate to make the people holy through His own blood." According to this scripture, through the blood of our Lord Jesus Christ, I am sanctified (made holy) and set apart for God.

- Declaration 5: 1 Corinthians 6:19–20 states, "Do you not know that your body is a temple of the Holy Spirit, who is in you, whom you have received from God? You are not your own; you were bought at a price. Therefore honor God with your body." According to this scripture, my body is a temple of the Holy Spirit, redeemed, cleansed, and sanctified by the blood of my Lord Jesus Christ. Therefore, Satan has no place in my life and no power over me or anything that concerns me through the blood of our Lord Jesus Christ.[35]

Yoga

Some churches have started accepting yoga and even offer yoga classes to their members. They are offered as fitness classes. What many do not realize is that yoga evolved from Hinduism. *The Merriam-Webster Dictionary* defines yoga as "a Hindu theistic philosophy teaching the suppression of all activity of body, mind and will in order that the self may realize its distinction from them and attain liberation." An additional definition is "a system of physical postures, breathing techniques and sometimes meditation derived from yoga but often practiced independently, especially in Western cultures, to promote physical and emotional well-being."[36] Yoga is a significant part of the Hindu's spiritual journey, and it is an enabler in the pursuit of Moksha. Each posture in yoga has a deep significance. We need to understand the context, origins and be respectful of them.

Angels

Ever since I was a child, I have been fascinated by angels. The Holy Scriptures talk about them extensively. They were present during the announcement of the birth of our Lord Jesus Christ (Luke 2), they comforted Him in the Garden of Gethsemane (Luke 22:43), and they were present at the announcement of the Resurrection when the angels rolled away the stone that sealed the tomb of our Lord Jesus Christ (Matthew 28:2). "There was a violent earthquake, for an angel of the Lord came down from heaven and, going to the tomb, rolled back the stone and sat on it." They were present at the time of His Ascension in Acts 1:9–11 when the disciples were looking skyward as our Lord was taken up.

We read about two prominent angels in the Holy Scriptures, one being Gabriel and the other being Michael. Of the two, only Michael is referred to as the archangel (Jude 1:9). Recently I was in conversation with a man who was convinced that an angel helped his daughter when she was lost in a new place and had lost her way. John Calvin writes,

> Angels are dispensers of divine beneficence to us.
> But the point on which the scriptures specially

insist is that which tends most to our comfort, and to the confirmation of our faith, namely, that angels are the ministers and dispensers of the divine bounty towards us. Accordingly, we are told how they watch for our safety, how they undertake our defence, direct our path, and take heed that no evil befall us.[37]

Calvin also points out that the Holy God delegates angels to protect those whom He has undertaken to protect. In Matthew 26:53, our Lord Jesus Christ asks His disciples a question at the time of His arrest when one of them resorted to violence. "Do you think I cannot call on my Father, and He will at once put at my disposal more than twelve legions of angels?" We need to keep in mind that angels are subject to and operate at the command of the Holy God. They have no independent operating authority. It is legitimate to ask the Holy God for angelic protection as our Lord showed, but they must not be worshipped or glorified.

The Rev. Dr. Billy Graham, in his book *Angels*, talks about his personal belief in them. Defending his view, he said that the Holy Scriptures talk about the existence of angels, and he believed the Holy Scriptures to be the true Word of God. He also testified that he had sensed the presence of angels on special occasions.[38]

In our culture, with the great focus on the satanic and demonic, even to a point of romanticization in popular culture, little is said about angels. In Hebrews 1:14, angels are called "ministering spirits." My favorite instances of angelic assistance as described in the Holy Scriptures are the following:

- An angel went before the servant of Abraham as he set out on the important mission of finding a bride for Isaac (Genesis 24:7).
- An angel is promised to be with the servant of Abraham as he undertakes and completes the mission that was assigned to him

(Genesis 24:40). In Exodus 23:20, there is a similar assurance. "See I am sending an angel ahead of you to guard you along the way and to bring you to the place I have prepared."

- Angels were also sent to provide directional guidance. The Holy God sent an angel to block Balaam's path in Numbers 22:22.

- Angels have assisted in individual worship and enhanced the quality of worship, as we find in the case of Manoah and his wife in Judges 13:19–20. Here, an angel was sent by the Holy God to perform what the Holy Scriptures report as "an amazing thing."

- In 2 Chronicles 32:21, angelic protection is offered in the face of overwhelming opposition. In this instance, the Holy God sent an angel to decimate the forces of an opposing army. In Psalm 34:7, this assurance is given: "The angel of the Lord encamps around those who fear Him, and delivers them." Additionally, Psalm 91:11–12 says, "For He will command His angels concerning your ways; they will lift you up in their hands, so that you will not strike your foot against a stone." This is personalized protection at its best.

- Angels have also been sent to assist humans in times of great fear. Luke 1:13 reports that the Holy God sent an angel who assures Zachariah during his time of great fear. In fact, that was the message of the Angel Gabriel to Mary, the Mother of our Lord, in Luke 1:30.

- There is a record in John 5:4 where it is mentioned that an angel was sent to the pool at Bethesda to stir up the waters, and anyone who went into the water first was healed of whatever disease they had. In times of sickness, angels have been sent to carry the Holy God's healing power.

- Our Lord also mentions the angels as witnesses and cheerleaders when a single sinner repents in Luke 15:10. "In the same way, I tell you, there is great rejoicing in the presence of the angels of God over one sinner who repents."

Conclusion and Prayer

Being a faithful follower of our Lord Jesus Christ does not mean one mountaintop experience after another. There will be sorrows, heartbreak, opposition, and unfairness that will be thrown our way in a fallen, dysfunctional world. The Holy Scriptures do not assure us that we will be kept from any suffering but that the Holy God Himself will be with us in our suffering, including some of the darkest and loneliest times. In fact, our Lord counseled in John 16:33 that, if we are in this world, we will have trouble and difficulty. Paul, in 2 Timothy 3:12, emphatically states, "Everyone who wants to live a godly life in Christ Jesus will be persecuted." Dietrich Bonhoeffer, who died a martyr, was on point when he said, "Suffering is the badge of true discipleship."[39]

> Holy God, thank You for holding every day in the life of _____ in the palms of Your hands. The Holy Scriptures assure us that our tears and fears matter to You, and we are assured of Your unwavering presence amid the storms we face. When_____ walks through trials and sufferings, may You reveal Yourself to him/her and walk alongside as _____ walks through every scary moment in life. I pray that You will help him/her look back on the numerous times in the past when You have been the rescuer _____, believing that all things work for the ultimate good of those who trust You. Give _____ clarity and strength, and may his/her faith be strengthened. May _____ see Your presence more clearly than the opposing forces and enemies surrounding him/her, realizing that Your power and protection are present and more powerful. I pray for healing of bodies and

minds, encouragement, and perseverance. And when _____ feels weak, lost or emotionally paralyzed, I pray that You will carry him/her. May God the Holy Spirit be the comforter and intercessor for _____. I pray that every evil force, satanic involvement, and demonic oppression be neutralized and defeated in and through the Holy Blood of our Lord Jesus Christ that was shed for _____ on Calvary. May _____ see Your amazing work and glorify Your Holy name. I pray this prayer in the name of Your Holy Son and our Lord Jesus Christ. Amen.

Prayer Markers: Challenges/Sufferings

On this day [date]	I prayed for

On this day [date]	I prayed for

On this day [date]	I prayed for

CHAPTER FOUR

Companions

B OB (NOT HIS REAL NAME) EXCITEDLY EXPLAINED TO ME HOW one of the young men he was mentoring had made great progress in straightening out his life and how Bob was providing all the support he could to the make this happen. I was very enthusiastic at the prospect of this young man making an impact, given the challenging circumstances of his life. I did not hear from Bob for a couple of weeks, and when I did, he told me that this young man, who was on the verge of doing something wonderful with his life, had returned to his old friends and was subsequently killed in a shootout.

Friends play such an important part in the lives of our children, and over the years I have sat with heartbroken parents who tearfully explained how the lives of their children were ruined by bad company. This being true, why not title this chapter "Friends"? My purpose in titling it "Companions" is to widen the scope of our prayers to include life partners and social support networks in our children's later years.

Growing up, I did not always have the benefit of good friends. As a result, from time to time, I got into bad company. My mother quite often would warn me about bad company. Of course, at that time, I could not hear her wisdom and was angered at what seemed to be a very judgmental attitude toward my friends. In hindsight, when I saw the outcome of bad company both in my own life and in the lives of others, I knew she was right. My mother fervently prayed for good influences in my life, and friends were significant contributors to that.

In most homes, discussions around the bad influence of friends rarely go well. While admittedly there are other things that we can do, it is my view that much of our effort will have to be in prayer. We must start praying from the time children are born. It has been my experience that at the point when most individuals realize the impact that bad company has had on them, some of the best opportunities of their lives have passed them by.

The apostle Paul, writing to the Corinthian church in 1 Corinthians 15:33, says, "Do not be misled: Bad company corrupts good character." *The Moody Bible Commentary,* expounding on this verse, points out that "bad company" could include those who denied the resurrection or simply keeping the company of bad doctrine.[40]

The Holy Scriptures describe a beautiful friendship in Daniel 3:16–28. Scholars view the time frame as some years after Daniel interpreted the king's dream. Three friends—Shadrach, Meshach, and Abednego—were put to a loyalty test. I have read of a couple of reasons why this was necessary, the first being that a revolt was against King Nebuchadnezzar and this was a test of loyalty to him. The other reason, suggested by Don Fleming in his *Concise Bible Commentary,* is that Babylon was a nation of many races, religions, and languages and in a plan designed to create "unity," Nebuchadnezzar had a statue erected.[41] It is also said that he did not have the statue installed in the capital but in the plains of Dura. Leaders and officials from across the land were invited to pay homage to the statue, and details of worship were provided to them. Shadrach, Meshach, and Abednego had been recommended by Daniel for their current positions per chapter 2 of Daniel, and my supposition is that Daniel must have had substantial influence on their lives, teaching them to be strong in resisting idolatry.

Imagine a huge gathering including many of great importance attending from far and wide. And at that gathering, when everyone fell and worshipped the image, three young men, probably in their early teens, were the only ones standing. These brilliant young men were fully aware of the consequences of their action, yet they stood their ground, and their act is recorded for posterity. I recently read that unearthed clay tablets seem to mention the names of Shadrach, Meshach, and Abednego in a list of nobility. I often think of these youngsters away from their homes, facing a test of faith. I am sure they must have had conversations among themselves before or after their disobedient act.

Sometimes when our children are faced with such tests of loyalty, they are away from their homes, and the only support they can count on will be their friends. The book *Extreme Devotion,* published by the Voice of the Martyrs, includes a story of four young Sudanese boys who were tortured for their faith. They were asked to renounce our Lord Jesus Christ, even as the blood was pouring out of their tortured bodies and they were screaming for their mothers in pain. Yet they refused to renounce their faith.

The Holy Scriptures provide outstanding examples of friendship, both good and bad. It is amazing how it is applicable to every stage of our lives.

Selection of Friends

This is one of the most difficult growth steps in a child's life. We must pray that God will orchestrate the right kind of friendships in their lives. We need to pray that they will select friends who will enrich their lives, not diminish them.

I am fascinated by the accuracy of the psalms as they represent every state of the human heart. In Psalm 70, King David writes about two groups of people. First, he describes those who are out to shame him and discredit him and even want to take his life. The other group consists of those who seek God, rejoice, are glad in God, love His salvation, and exalt God. These are the people we should pray our children will meet and with whom they will develop friendships. Friends can add value to the spiritual, physical, and mental growth of individuals. Sometimes children will need more of a mentoring relationship like Timothy had with Paul.

I have often wondered what life was like for kids who came out of Egypt and traveled to the Promised Land. In Exodus 2, Moses is introduced, and the historical account is given of his adoption into the Egyptian palace. In verse 11, the Holy Scriptures record, "One day after Moses had grown up," he went to see his people. In Acts 7:23, we read, "When Moses was forty years old, he decided to visit his fellow Israelites." Acts 7:22 tells us that while growing up in the palace, "Moses was educated in all the wisdom of the Egyptians and was powerful in speech, and action." Did Moses make friends during that time? How was he treated by the other kids in the palace? We can only guess, but what is evident is that his faith in the God of his birth parents was not diminished or replaced.

Once our children leave home, they will make friendships, finding friends who could potentially have a greater influence than we as parents or sponsors can. We must pray that those friendships will only strengthen their faith.

Another timeless example of strong friendship given to us in the Holy Scriptures is that of David and Jonathan. David had become a member of Saul's household and was a fierce warrior who had won many victories. Jonathan was one of the sons of Saul. We read about their friendship in 1 Samuel 20 and 1 Samuel 23:15–18. Some takeaways and prayer points include the following:

- There was no jealousy in their friendship. Though Jonathan was the son of Saul, he was not jealous of David's future role as king. The pressure that our children face, and will face increasingly as they grow up, will only be compounded by friends who are jealous of them.

- They treated each other as equals and were respectful of each other. Once David was aware that he was going to be the king, he could have taken a controlling or domineering stance in the relationship. I have been with parents who have pleaded helplessness in the face of domineering or controlling friends.
- They did not use each other, nor did they demean each other. When David came to Jonathan for help in 1 Samuel 20, his reaction was not judgmental or advisory; instead, he responded to David's need with assurance and action. It was a growth-oriented friendship as they matured in life, and as their friendship matured, their own faith journey progressed as well.

I recommend fasting and praying for the selection of good friends beginning at the time children are born and continuing at every major transition, such as from playschool to preschool, elementary to middle school, middle school to high school, high school to university, university to a job, and even when they relocate. When I accepted the Lord Jesus Christ as my personal Lord and Savior as a teenager, I was introduced to a group of friends who were new believers like me. They supported my growth and development as a Christian, and we helped each other in our Christian walk. In Ecclesiastics 4:10, King Solomon writes, "If one falls down, his friend can help him up. But pity the man who falls and has no one to help him up." God had gifted each of us very differently, and although we were raw and inexperienced, God used us. We went out and had a lot of fun like all teenagers do, but our faith and walk with Christ was so much enhanced.

Ashok was the de facto leader. Ashok met God through exceedingly difficult circumstances. In Ashok's life, I could see the miraculous restoration of a life that was completely shattered socially, physically, and emotionally. Ashok, Arun, and Thomas were part of the core group that helped me in my faith formation. We had little money or resources, but we were ready to take all our imperfections to a perfect God and let Him use us. God did just that, and we shared the gospel with everyone who cared to listen. We traveled miles on our bicycles, singing and sharing the gospel in villages. The message was amazingly simple. As Martin Luther put it, "We were beggars telling other beggars where to find food." We checked on each other's Bible reading and prayer, we fasted, and we met for all-night prayer. It was as if our lives were so parched that we could not get enough of the living waters of our Lord Jesus Christ.

It was on one such occasion that Ashok excitedly announced that we were going to have a new member—Samuel—who was a student from Nigeria. Imagine meeting and fellowshipping with an African in southern India. Sam was 100 percent African, and he took our relationship with our Lord Jesus Christ to a different level altogether. Today there is so much talk about diversity, including the need for it. When we seek God and His Word, He will always bring diversity into the group. Our lives have taken different twists and turns, but we keep in touch more than forty-five years later. Every time we have a chance to meet, we still pray together and check on each other's walk with our Lord Jesus Christ.

A while ago, I was at the funeral of a lady who had two sons. The elder, after a dispute with his younger brother over money, had left home twenty-five years prior. The prodigal son was so mad that he cut all ties with the family and had no contact with them. This lady was hoping that somehow she would be able to see her older son before she died, but it never happened. A relationship among siblings can be one of contention, confrontation, and complete devastation of the family relationship. This frequently happens in Christian families. When our Lord Jesus Christ related the story of the prodigal son, while much of the focus admittedly is on the younger son, the parable provides a wealth of lessons on family relationships. Take the relationship between the two brothers. Surely the older brother picked up much of the slack after the younger brother left. It might have been financial, physical, or emotional, or perhaps he was the one who supported their parents as they picked up the pieces of their lives after the departure of his brother. However, when his brother returned and he saw the restoration of his status, he was neither excited nor happy.

In the very first book of the Holy Bible, Genesis, we read the account of Cain and Abel (chapter 4), the story of Esau and Jacob (chapter 27), and the report of the jealousy of Joseph's brothers (chapter 37). Of course, the argument can be made that the parents were culpable in fueling each situation. David seemed to have had a good relationship with his parents and his siblings, but even he in Psalm 69:8 laments, "I am a stranger to my brothers, and an alien to my own mother's sons." The phrase "Blood is thicker than water," although used to indicate that family relationships are stronger that others, is not in the Holy Bible.

The Holy Bible is replete with examples of sibling hatred and other family relationship issues. In Genesis, we read about the dispute between Abraham and Lot in chapter 13, primarily over land or property. Sadly, many Christian families today are experiencing serious conflict because of property, finances, and other material disputes between siblings or even between parents and children. Satan does his best to effectively use property and other material possessions to drive a wedge between professing Christians. In other family relationships, this is evident as well; Abraham stepped back and let his nephew Lot take the best of the land, as Genesis 13:8–9 recorded.

> So Abram said to Lot, "Let's not have any quarrelling between you and me, or between your herdsmen and mine, for we are brothers [brethren]. Is not the whole land before you? Let's part company. If you go to the left, I will go to the right. If you go to the right, I'll go to the left."

Abraham gave Lot the choice, and Abraham was rewarded for that action by God Himself. My point is unless we pray for family relationships—especially those between siblings and between children and parents—they may fracture under the stress of Satan's attacks. I recommend that parents start praying for sibling relationships from the time the second child is conceived, if not earlier, and for good relationships between the parents and children from the time the first child is conceived.

The Influence of Friends

In 1 Kings 12, we read an account of a disastrous influence of friends. After the death of Solomon, the people made an earnest request of Rehoboam, Solomon's son and successor king. They wanted relief from some of the conditions his father had placed on them. Rehoboam was about to be crowned king, and the people were asking for some leniency in their hard service in return for their loyalty. Some Bible scholars point out that Solomon had taken on some overly ambitious building projects for which he was taxing the citizens with both labor and money. The weary people now requested that the new king show some kindness. It is interesting that the delegation of the people's representatives was led by Jeroboam, the son of Nebat, who had rebelled against Solomon and now had returned from Egypt where he had fled. The story is told in 1 Kings 12. Not only was Rehoboam being tested for his leadership but also for his wisdom as a problem-solver. Holding off the request by asking for some time, Rehoboam consulted two sets of people. The first had been the advisors of his father, King Solomon, and the second were some of Rehoboam's friends who had grown up with him. He rejected the advice of the advisors and accepted the advice of his friends (1 Kings 12:10–11) with disastrous consequences. Rehoboam was forty-one years old at this critical juncture of his life (1 Kings 14:21). We read in 1 Kings 12:8, "But Rehoboam rejected the advice the elders gave him and consulted the young men who had grown up with him and were serving him." The obvious fact is these friends had had a long and lasting influence on Rehoboam. We need to pray fervently and specifically about the influence that friends have over the lives of our children. They have the potential of lasting impact on the following:

- Children themselves. At forty-one years of age, Rehoboam was dependent on his friends to make a decision of great magnitude. His father's wisdom had obviously not rubbed off on him. I would hazard a guess that if he was not influenced by his friends, after discussing the matter with both groups, he would have decided on his own or arrived at a decision that was a hybrid of both opinions. Presumably, he was accustomed to having his friends' acceptance and approval in every decision he made. Succumbing to the desperate need for approval and acceptance, even if it means surrendering their own individuality, faith foundations, and upbringing, is particularly important to pray against on behalf of our children. In Rehoboam's case, this unhealthy dependence crushed any show of creativity and portrayed the new king as someone who was out of touch with reality. His familiarity with his friends made him turn to them for advice for a matter in which they had no competence or background. Our children should not miss God's plan and purpose for their lives by heeding the advice of their friends. In Proverbs 1:5, Solomon wrote, "Let the wise listen and add to their learning, and let the discerning get guidance." We should pray that our children listen and learn but decide independently in consultation with God.
- Closest relationships. When our children are influenced by domineering and alienating friends, there could be an impact on the children's closest relationships. It is unclear what type of relationship Rehoboam had with Jeroboam up to this point, but it did not improve from that point forward. First Kings 14:30 indicates there was continual

warfare between him and Jeroboam. I have sat with parents whose children do not have a line of communication with them because they are so influenced by their friends. In addition, Rehoboam sent out Adoniram for damage control, and he was stoned to death by the people (1 Kings 12:18–19). A mutual and reciprocal influence will only enhance the quality of life and enrich the relationships that the child is part of. Most critically, Rehoboam's act also resulted in the division of the kingdom, and he was left with only two tribes to rule over while Jeroboam took ten. Rehoboam lost the empire and his future when he was influenced by the counsel of his friends. The result was permanent damage. If our children subject themselves to the wrong counsel, they can permanently damage relationships, erase everything that has been handed down to them, and even lose a promising future. I have been awestruck to see tightknit families completely torn apart because of one child and in only one generation. No God-centered family can presume a good relationship with and among the children. Unity is one of the key elements that Satan attacks.

- Larger relationships. The larger circle of people who depended on Rehoboam's leadership was also impacted by his decision. At forty-one years old, he was a disaster. It is not only our younger children who need prayers; sometimes the older ones are susceptible to poor decisions influenced by friends as well. I believe that sometimes this could also be manifested in an irresponsible lifestyle. Proverbs 11:29 warns, "He who brings trouble on his family will inherit only wind." I like the explanation provided by *The Moody Bible Commentary* for this verse. "This proverb probably profiles a foolish son. He troubles his family, his own house, whether by bad decisions, wasting resources, alienating relationships, turning away from the Lord or something else. As a result, he will inherit the wind—that is, nothing."[42]

While it is important for our children to have friends, it takes focused, persistent prayer to ensure that Satan does not interfere and derail them from, as William Carey said, "expecting great things from God and attempting great things for God."[43]

Life Partners

His name was Abraham, and from the time when he was a little boy, his mother prayed for his life partner. During one of her prayer sessions, this mother was impressed by one feminine name. She continued praying for many years till Abraham was ready to be married. As was the most prevalent custom of the time, his parents started suggesting potential brides for him. There was one girl that Abraham really liked, but she was introduced by a name other than the one his mother had prayed about. It then turns out this young woman's middle name was the one his mother had received during her prayer time when he was a little boy. My point is that we should start praying for the life partners of children when they are incredibly young.

Imagine that, around the time a child is born, there could be another child born earlier or later who could be the potential life partner according to God's plan. How wonderful it would be for two sets of parents to be praying for someone else's child who they do not even know but will meet years later. As the years progress in the child's life, these prayers could be more tailored to the personality of the child. God in His mercy and goodness will prepare the other child to be the "customized" life partner. I am not in any way suggesting that their marriage will be completely devoid of struggles or challenges. The foundation would be on the individual customization carried out by God. In this process, we need to pray that our children will wait until the individual selected by God will be revealed.

Let us examine the opposite of such a God-ordained union, which would look something like this: the child drifting in and out of multiple relationships and, even unwittingly, letting their past relationships influence the next one. Of course, the Holy Bible is noticeably clear regarding followers of our Lord Jesus Christ marrying unbelievers. When this happens, there is usually a compromise in which one wedding ceremony is conducted according to the religion of the nonfollower and another Christian ceremony is also held. In my opinion, every religion is exclusive, and it does no justice to either of the religions to engage in such a compromise. Additionally, it goes against the grain of the first commandment for the follower.

I have also seen a practice, with which I also disagree, in which the nonfollower converts to Christianity for the sole purpose of getting married in a church or to have the marriage blessed by a Christian priest. Christianity has no meaning outside of a relationship with our Lord Jesus Christ. It also needs to be kept in mind that in some religions, sons perform the final religious rites of their parents, and they cannot do that if they have converted to another religion.

When our son-in-law, Matt, asked for the hand of our daughter, Nandy, I had a long discussion with him on his relationship with our Lord Jesus Christ. In addition, I also requested that our senior pastor have a conversation with him. Enquiring about the spiritual life of a potential spouse on behalf of one's child is a responsibility that parents need to take very seriously. It must be a done in love and with genuine care.

Later Life Companionship

I saw a movie that portrayed a husband and wife who, after many years of marriage, passed on only a few hours from one another. I would say this is the best-case scenario. For years, I have volunteered in an Alzheimer's support group for caregivers. Also, as a church elder, I have visited the homes of those who are older. I have often been struck by the lack of support these individuals are given. As our years advance, our journey sometimes becomes lonelier and our bodies become weaker. In his book *The Grand Weaver*, Ravi Zacharias points out,

> God does not display His work in abstract terms.
> He prefers the concrete, and this means that at the
> end of your life one of the three things will happen
> to your heart: it will grow hard, it will be broken,
> or it will be tender.[44]

Whatever happens to older adults' hearts during their later years, we should pray that the God who cares about their grievances, hurts, and regrets will send them support, companionship, and encouragement in their final years.

Conclusion and Prayer

Companions significantly impact the lives of our children. We need to pray that in a world of social media and virtual friendships, our children will be open to invest in friendships that add value to their lives. Choosing and investing in friends who will build them up and not tear them down will require courage in our children. We need to support them with our prayers as they make such decisions. Sometimes, even when individuals decide to walk away from negative friendships, it is not uncommon for those friends to pursue them or somehow try to reenter their lives. When we pray that the Holy God will save them from negative friendships, we should also pray that they will be given the strength to make a clean break and not have any lingering links. The Holy God will also have to give our children the strength to wait for the right life partner and to be able to recognize the Holy God's choice for them. Finally, how wonderful it will be if our children are blessed with the support of a peer group in their evening years.

> Holy God, I pray that You will provide healthy,
> positive   friendships   for   _____
> throughout his/her life. May _____ be

blessed with friendships that build, support, and enhance his/her faith. I pray that _____ will invest in deep, lasting friendships that are pleasing to You. Please lead _____ to friends that You have selected for him/her. When it is time to move away from friendships that are not pleasing in Your sight, please give _____ the strength to make that decision quickly and to completely let go. I pray that You will grant patience and determination to _____ to wait for Your guidance and direction in the choice of his/her life partner. Fill _____ with joy, self-control, and contentment during that time of waiting. Please bless and prepare the life partner that You have chosen for _____. Please eliminate loneliness, establish a family, bless their relational intimacy, and give them the strength to keep all of the sacred vows made before You. In Your time of choosing, may You bless them with children. Please bless, protect, and enrich his/her marriage every day and protect it from any disfunction through the blood of our precious Lord that was shed for the two of them on Calvary. Help them to be teachable and not self-centered, and may their love for each other never wane or grow cold no matter how imperfect they may find each other. May You show mercy and favor in his/her evening years and provide a wonderful support network. May _____ find incredible joy and purpose in the life that You have intended for him/her. I pray this prayer in the name of Your Holy Son and our Lord Jesus Christ. Amen.

Prayer Markers: Companions

On this day [date]	I prayed for

On this day [date]	I prayed for

CHAPTER FIVE

Character

I T IS NOT UNCOMMON EVERY DAY TO HEAR ABOUT SOME LEADER who is exposed for character flaws, so much so that a newspaper columnist commented that identifying character failures among professing evangelical leaders is like shooting fish in a barrel. Many years ago, a pastor from a particular denomination was convinced that I should consider going to the seminary. He invited me to his office to discuss it, and as soon as I settled into a chair in his office, I noticed a strange picture on the wall. It was of his seminary graduating class, and he had X marks drawn beside the faces of about half the class, if not more. My curiosity got the better of me, and I asked him what the X's signified. He explained that they were either ousted from the ministry for character issues or left on their own.

This disheartening example holds true not only in the case of ministry but also in every walk of life. Dallas Willard, in his book *Renovation of the Heart*, argues,

The revolution of Jesus in the first place and continuously is a revolution of the human heart or spirit. It does not proceed by means of the formation of social institutions and laws, the outer forms of existence, intending that these would then impose a good order of life upon people who come under their power. Rather, His is a revolution of character which proceeds by changing people from the inside out through an ongoing personal relationship to God in Christ and to one another. It is one that changes their ideas, beliefs, feelings, and habits of choice as well as their bodily tendencies and social relations. It penetrates to the deepest layers of their souls.[45]

Character must be rooted and grounded in a relationship with our Lord Jesus Christ to develop and thrive. This enables consistency of thought and action.

Many years ago, when we first arrived in the US from India, we took a road trip along with some close family members, visiting five or six states. Around nightfall, we pulled into a place of interest. The place had an entry fee, but there was no one on duty to enforce it. Placed near the entrance was a transparent box with money in it, and apparently those who had visited before us had dropped their entrance fees in the box even though no one was watching. Such actions required some level of human decency, thus good character.

So for what character traits should we be praying in our children? Without doubt, most Christians would point to the fruit of the Spirit delineated in Galatians 5:22–23. "But the fruit of the Spirit is love, joy, peace, patience, kindness, goodness, faithfulness, gentleness and self-control." *The Moody Bible Commentary* suggests that Paul, in this passage, is talking about virtues that every follower of our Lord Jesus Christ must actively pursue and the dependence on the help of God the Holy Spirit in that pursuit.[46]

If one closely examined the list provided by Paul, it should be clear that most if not all relate to how we treat others. On further examination, I discovered that Bible scholars list more character traits found in the Holy Bible. When I tried to consolidate a list, there were over one hundred. Some of them extrapolated the character traits of our Lord Jesus Christ from His life on earth, including serving, pointing out that our Lord Jesus Christ was the ultimate servant.

Over the years, I have watched the struggles of followers of our Lord Jesus Christ, sometimes even to the point of completely giving up. I have also been a keen student of reasons why the world is so cynical about the Christian faith. One world leader said, "Christians are ordinary people making extraordinary claims." Another said, "If it weren't for Christians, I would be a Christian."

In years past, the practice regarding Christian confirmation included the officiating bishop first questioning each of the confirmation candidates individually to determine whether they were ready to be confirmed. It was also a practice for the bishop to address the candidates with a special message. The bishop who confirmed my group of confirmands said that our lives would be the only gospel that a lot of people would read. I have over the years realized how true this statement is in the multicultural context in which we live.

In my extensive travels, I have concluded that to be an effective follower of our Lord Jesus Christ, people need to see a holistic demonstration of different character traits as each situation demands. I took my daughter, then a high school senior, to a different country where she was to intern with a relief organization. She was assigned to work with a group of children who were in a halfway home. It was hot and humid, and one of the very thirsty children ran to an outside water faucet to drink. Apparently, it was not the scheduled time when those kids were permitted to drink water, and consequently, the child was beaten with a stick by one of the staff. My daughter watched this and defended the little boy, complaining about the behavior of the staff member. Here she clearly demonstrated a couple of character traits: first, compassion for the boy, and second, the courage to stand up for him.

I have assembled a list of what I consider to be the top nine character traits that we should be praying for in our children. This is by no means an exhaustive list; it is only devised through the lens of my own experience:

1. Faith

Faith is an essential ingredient in the life of a follower of our Lord Jesus Christ. I have often wondered what is meant by "having faith," as it is commonly described. Is it something that a person puts on in the face of troubles or difficulties and continues to amplify as the troubles and difficulties intensify?

I have often heard people talk about needing more faith or lacking in faith. Is faith an excuse to remain stubborn while getting what an individual desires? In some of the most difficult circumstances in my life, I have often wondered if my faith is strong enough. Or is my inadequate faith somehow a hinderance for a Holy God to intervene in my circumstances and deliver me?

In 2 Corinthians 5:7, Paul confirms, "We live by faith, not by sight." In my simplistic mind, I have often wondered whether to start walking by faith when I am faced with troubles and difficulties. Or is it true faith to walk continuously, daily in all aspects of my life, be they large or small?

The writer of Hebrews, in chapter 11, provides a list of great examples of people who have become known as "Heroes of Faith." This chapter seems to discuss the outcome of faith rather that what faith exactly was for each of them. But one thing appears evident. Faith was a lifestyle for those described there. It did not appear to be something that they put on from time to time. Examining their lives, an overly simplistic definition of faith could be something like this:

Faith is a lifestyle devoted to dependence on, obedience to, and worship of the Holy God, anchored in trust in His promises, the confidence that He is powerful, faithful, and—despite any obvious evidence in my current circumstance or hardships in the short term—the unshakable hope and assurance that the Holy God will reward me and deliver on His promises in a timeline of His choosing, keeping my best interests in His loving heart.

A person who adopts a lifestyle of faith knows that the Holy God will prevail. He always does, and He always has. Being faithful to the Holy God is a journey of a lifetime. I often reflect on the farewell message of Joshua, recorded in Joshua 23:14. Joshua testifies to the faithfulness of the Holy God, saying, "Now I am about to go the way of all the earth. You know with all your heart and soul that not one of all the good promises the Lord your God gave you has failed. Every promise has been fulfilled; not one has failed." What a brilliant testimony at the end of his life, which was anything but peaceful or painless.

2. Credibility

As a researcher in leadership, I have read about the importance of credibility in leadership. Entire books have written on the topic. *The Merriam-Webster Dictionary* defines *credibility* as "the quality or power of inspiring belief." Another definition is "the quality of being believable or worthy of trust." Some of the other definitions cite trustworthiness, reliability, dependability, and integrity as traits of being credible.[47] I suggest that if life consists of reciprocal relationships, then the results are directly proportionate to what we invest in them.

Credible lives build credible relationships. One such life described in the Holy Scriptures is that of Joseph in Genesis 37–47. What an incredible life! Joseph was loved by his father, hated and almost killed by his brothers, sold into slavery, incarcerated, falsely accused, mistreated, gracious to pass up an opportunity for revenge, and helpful to those who had harmed him. Yet he was deserving of the trust and confidence of those whose encountered him. He was reliable and did what he said he would do, when he said he would do it.

Credible people are those on whom others can depend. They take responsibility for their actions. James Kouzes and Barry Posner, in their book *Credibility: How Leaders Gain and Lose It, Why People Demand It*, propose,

> Credibility, like reputation, is something that is earned over time. It does not come automatically with a job or the title. It begins early in our lives and careers. People tend to assume initially that someone who has risen to a certain status in life, acquired degrees, or achieved significant goals is deserving of their confidence. But complete trust is granted (or not) only after people have had the chance to get the know more about the person. The credibility foundation is built brick by brick. And as each new fragment is secured, the basis on which we can erect the hopes of the future is gradually built.[48]

We need to pray that our children will have the credibility of Joseph.

3. Treatment of Others

The apostle Paul, in his letter to the Galatians, verses 5:22–23, talks about the fruits of the Spirit being "love, joy, peace, patience, kindness, goodness, faithfulness, gentleness and self-control." Explaining this exhortation, *The Moody Bible Commentary,* while emphasizing that Paul is not suggesting a life of passivity but one of active pursuit that is aided and directed by God the Holy Spirit, goes on to provide explanations for some of the fruit.

- Love. This is a big challenge. The original word that Paul uses to describe God's love toward human beings denotes a kind of constant, nonvariable love even in the case of those who are seemingly unlovable. We are quick to tolerate people, but that is not what the demand is.
- Joy. When I was a little boy in Sunday school, we sang a song that went something like this: "Jesus first, yourself last, and others in between." Joy is not dependent on the circumstances in which we find ourselves.
- Patience. This is lived out in bearing with difficult people or situations while maintaining one's composure.
- Self-control. This means restraint, holding oneself back from acting on evil desires and relationships.
- Kindness. We are kind when we act in gracious or generous ways.
- Gentleness. We exhibit gentleness when we use the least amount of force or power necessary when dealing with people. I see this as knowing one's strength or advantage over the weakness of another yet deciding not to use it.
- Goodness. In my view, gentleness is purity of thought, motive and action while not expecting any reward or recognition.[49]

No amount of training, systems, deterrents, or shaming will ensure our treatment of others. What seems to a recent trend regarding this topic is the idea that we should make sure some races are shamed into thinking that being born into their race was somehow an error. If we buy into that theory, then we assume that the Holy God when creating us made a mistake in our race assignment.

In Galatians 5:18, Paul writes about being "led by the Spirit." Being led means making progress, following, and walking one step at a time. We cannot do this in our own strength. A follower of our Lord Jesus Christ who is led by God the Holy Spirit treats others not from a position of weakness or vulnerability but from a position of strength. We do this fully aware of our ability to do significant damage to others yet refraining from doing so because we are led by God the Holy Spirit. We as humans can do significant damage to others. When we walk with God the Holy Spirit and treat others per that guidance, we leave the results to the Holy God.

In the psalms, David laments to the Holy God about how people have been treating him: friends' betrayal of him and even his desire for revenge. A follower of our Lord Jesus Christ expresses his or her genuine feelings to the Holy God about how others have been treating them and hand over to Him any desire for revenge or retaliation. Romans 12:19 instructs, "Do not take revenge, my friends, but leave room for God's wrath, for it is written: 'It is mine to avenge; I will repay,' says the Lord."

We must pray that our children seek the leading of God the Holy Spirit in their treatment of others.

4. Self-Control

As I write this book, there is a growing list of preachers who have crashed and burned for lack of self-control. Some of them strode like giants in the world of Christianity. Some of them were people to whom I looked up and ardently followed. But I realized that standing amid all the failure and smoldering ashes is the singular figure of the cross. Anytime we take our focus off that cross, we will fall and fail. Self-control, from my perspective, is not being blinded, driven, or enslaved by our cravings and desires but disciplining, setting boundaries, and denying ourselves of instant or short-term gratification. Proverbs 25:28 states, "Like a city whose walls are broken down is a man who lacks self-control."

I have a niece, Erica, who swims at a collegiate and national collegiate level. I am amazed at the self-control she shows in her lifestyle. When a big competition is looming, her top priority objective is to keep herself fit and ready for the competition. She sets and adheres to boundaries and takes responsibility for what is within her boundaries. Self-control is developed as a way of life.

Henry Cloud and John Townsend in their book *Boundaries* speak to this.

> Boundaries help us to define our property so that we can take care of it. They help us to "guard our heart with all diligence." We need to keep things that will nurture us inside our fences and keep things that will harm us outside. In short, boundaries help keep the good in and the bad out.[50]

It is essentially deciding that there is a line that one will not cross. The authors then go on to discuss some common myths on setting boundaries, including perceiving that the one setting boundaries is being selfish, will hurt others, will be hurt by others, will burn bridges, or set boundaries that injure the individual.

In Paul's letter to Titus, 2:11–12, he explains,

> For the grace of God that brings salvation has appeared to all men. It teaches us to say "No" to ungodliness and worldly passions, and live self-controlled, upright and godly lives in this present age.

We can have self-control only when we look to the cross and ask for the grace of God to help us. We must pray that our children will seek God's grace to practice self-control.

5. Stewardship

I have lived and traveled extensively in the Middle East, and I have been fascinated by the people's efforts in transforming semi-arid, dry land into cultivatable land. My fascination was no less when I traveled this great land enjoying its forests, waterways, and breathtaking landscapes. It is almost a cliché to say that we should be stewards of what we use and enjoy for the benefit of those who come after us. We should cultivate a mindset of stewardship which, according to my belief, is taking care of something while it passes through us and leaving it in the same or improved condition.

Stewardship is a trust relationship. I have always been amazed at how specific the Holy Scriptures have been on various aspects of our lives. Leviticus 25:3–5 lays out notably clear instructions on treating the land.

> For six years sow your fields, and for six years prune your vineyards and gather their crops. But in the seventh year the land is to have a sabbath of rest, a sabbath to the Lord. Do not sow your fields or prune your vineyards.

In Job 12:7–10, it is made explicit.

> But ask the animals, and they will teach you, or the birds of the air, and they will tell you; or speak to the earth, and it will teach you, or let the fish of the sea inform you. Which of all these does not know that the hand of the Lord has done this? In his hand is the life of every creature.

Dr. Billy Graham said, "When we see the world as a gift from God, we will do our best to take care of it and use it wisely, instead of poisoning or destroying it." This also goes for our responsibilities as citizens of the country in which God placed us, such as staying informed, obeying laws, respecting authority, and getting involved in the community. No country is perfect or immune to the problems that plague society. It is our duty, and the duty of our children, to be good stewards and ensure that we leave what we hold temporarily in better condition for the next generation. We must pray that our children realize that we pass through this world only once and whatever we can do to help sustain and scale what we hold for a short time is good stewardship. It is only God who can help us maintain a balance between obsession and complete indifference.

6. Gratitude

Thomas Goodwin said, "Those blessings are sweetest that are won with prayer and worn with thanks." I never get tired of reading the story of the ten lepers in Luke 17:11–19. Every time I read it, I learn something new about the one leper who came back and thanked Jesus. He walked back alone, sought, and found our Lord Jesus Christ and thanked Him. Imagine the thoughts that were going through his mind as he walked back! I'm sure that there was joy on the face of the Savior; maybe even a smile broke out when He asked, "Were not all ten cleansed? Where are the other nine? Was no one found to return and give praise to God except this foreigner?" Imagine the joy, the excitement, of that leper. At that time, nothing else mattered to him; everything else could wait. He had to show his gratitude to the one who healed him.

The Holy Scriptures do not mention the age of this individual. WebMD.com states that children are more susceptible to leprosy than adults, so it is quite possible that he was in his teens. We are often like the other nine lepers who quickly moved on. They probably thought they could come back later to thank Jesus, but the Holy Scriptures do not ever record them meeting again. Upon realizing that he was healed, the leper took a pause and turned around to seek the One who healed him. His gratitude was immediate. He did not complain about all the years that he had missed due to his disease but was focused on the magnitude of what God did in that instance of his life: that day, that meeting, that miracle.

We should take "gratitude pauses" in our lives when we pause immediately and face God to thank Him for what he has done in our lives. We must show grateful spirits by example and pray that our children will have hearts of gratitude for even the smallest things they receive from God. There is no shortage of studies that show the positive effects of gratitude on the individual. Benefits include improved physical and mental health, better relationships, motivation, energy, and better moods.

Gratitude is also shown through appreciation in our interactions with others. My mother demonstrated this to me by always making it a point to thank people in person or write a note. I distinctly recall my meeting with a teacher at the parent/teacher conference of my daughter during her junior year in high school. I thanked the teacher for his hard work, and I asked him if my daughter was respectful and courteous to him. With tears pouring down his cheeks, he told me how encouraging it was to come across a parent who was appreciative.

I like the beginning of Ephesians 5:20, where Paul exhorts readers to "always give thanks." Always means in every instance—in *everything*. Again, Paul, in writing to the church in Thessalonica (1 Thessalonians 5:18), advises, "Give thanks in all circumstances." G. K. Chesterton said, "I would maintain that thanks are the highest form of thought, and that gratitude is happiness doubled by wonder."[51] We must pray that our children live life to the fullest and go through all the experiences that life will provide with a mindset of gratitude.

7. Contentment

The next character trait that I think is important for every child is contentment. In my view, every child faces so much social pressure to get the latest of everything or be unhappy and dissatisfied. There is a desire to always be one up on friends and classmates or even to *keep up with Joneses* when we grow up. Over the years, I have seen individuals who are never content with their lives and are constantly complaining, dissatisfied, envious, or under tremendous pressure to acquire more and more possessions. Their focus is always on what is lacking and how quickly it can be acquired. This lifestyle makes them miss much of the present or having an appreciation for what they have.

Contentment is a mindset that is based on the confidence that God has plans for me and He will add things to my life on His schedule, without impact to my personal peace. In Jeremiah 29:11, God promises, "'For I know the plans I have for you,' declares the Lord, 'plans to prosper you and not harm you, plans to give you hope and a future.'" God knows when we should have that car, house, or piece of furniture, and He will provide it not a day late. And in this hyperpressure environment in which our children grow up, only God can provide them with contentment.

In his first letter to Timothy, Paul writes, "But godliness with contentment is great gain" (1 Timothy 6:6). Every definition of *contentment* that I have read included satisfaction as its core component. In Hebrews 13:5, the writer provides an assurance. "Keep your lives free from the love of money and be content with what you have, because God has said, 'Never will I leave you; never will I forsake you.'"

It also must be clarified that there is a difference between contentment and laziness or complacency. The Holy Scriptures, while talking about contentment, also speak very strongly against laziness and complacency. If one were to juxtapose the biblical teachings on contentment with those on laziness and complacency, the difference appears to be that while one is content, individual effort, initiative, and improvement are not lacking; the outcome is left to God.

8. Work Ethic

It is my perspective that followers of our Lord Jesus Christ must have an exceedingly high work ethic and must be an example to others regardless of supervision or lack thereof. The Holy Scriptures speak of both men and women who served God while maintaining a profession of their own. The first to come to my mind is Lydia, who is mentioned in Acts 16:11–15. She was a cloth merchant who had become a follower of our Lord Jesus Christ. Warren Wiersbe, in his book *Life Sentences,* portrays Lydia as the most prominent of women who were being addressed by Paul. She was the wealthiest, coming from the city of Thyatira, famous for its purple cloth that was made into togas worn by Roman officials. Wiersbe goes on to speculate that she was probably a widow who was running her family business. Lydia's conversion also marked the beginning of the church in Philippi, according to Wiersbe. Acts 16:15 tells us that she invited Paul and his associates to stay in her home, indicating her belief in and wholehearted response to their teaching.

Paul's profession was equally impressive. In Acts 18:1–3, the Holy Scriptures confirm that Paul was a tentmaker and a great networker. Again, in Acts 20:34, Paul is quoted as saying, "You yourselves know that these hands of mine have supplied my own needs and the needs of my companions." In Exodus 20:9, God, when He gave the Ten Commandments to Moses, said, "Six days you shall labor and do all your work." During my years as a corporate professional, I have been disappointed by young people who I have helped to secure employment, to progress in their careers, or have mentored. These were usually raised in Christian homes yet had a remarkably bad work ethic. They were lazy, gave excuses, simply did not show up, or could not be trusted to do a job when unsupervised. What made it even more egregious was their proclamation to other employees that they were followers of our Lord Jesus Christ.

Whether in ministry or in a secular job, we should demonstrate an exceedingly high work ethic and be examples to others. Waiting on

God is not a license to be lazy or sloppy. Our value in the workplace is directly proportionate to our problem-solving abilities. In 2 Thessalonians 3:6–12, Paul powerfully makes a case against laziness and for a great work ethic. In verse 10, he states, "If a man will not work, he shall not eat." Again, in verse 11, he addresses the "busybodies." In a generic sense, busybodies can be defined as unsolicited meddlers in other people's affairs. We must pray that our children not only demonstrate an exceedingly high work ethic but also make a positive impact in the lives of those with whom they come into contact. Work happens in a social context. Modern organizations resemble societies more than archaic hierarchical structures. It is in this context that a follower of our Lord Jesus Christ can make a difference in the lives of his or her coworkers by being a "city on a hill."

It is also important that we pray for our children when they are in school and college.

9. Mental Toughness

Isaiah 50:7 is one of my favorite passages in the Holy Scriptures. "Because the Sovereign Lord helps me, I will not be disgraced. Therefore, have I set my face like a flint, and I will not be put to shame." Bible commentators postulate that Isaiah was prophesying about our Lord Jesus Christ and His perseverance despite hardship and opposition.

The organization Mental Toughness Inc. defines *mental toughness* as "the ability to resist, manage and overcome doubts, worries, concerns and circumstances that prevent you from succeeding or excelling at a task or towards an objective or a performance outcome that you set out to achieve."[52] This concept, I am told, was initially researched among athletes. No one demonstrated this more clearly than our Lord Jesus Christ. He was abandoned during the end of His earthly life, was lonely, was worried, and prayed at Gethsemane, where He sweat blood in His anguish. Hematidrosis is a rare condition, according to medical experts, in which an individual can sweat blood when under conditions of extreme stress, fear, anxiety, or fear of death. It is so intense that the capillaries around the sweat glands burst and blood oozes out as sweat. Despite all of this, the Lord Jesus Christ went ahead and did not sway from His objective.

Paul draws a parallel between the Christian life and that of an athlete. In 1 Corinthians 9:26, he paints the metaphor of a boxer who lands every foe with purpose and precision and a runner who runs to win the race. "Therefore, I do not run like a man running aimlessly; I do not fight like a man beating the air." Athletes deal with injuries, losses, fatigue, being overlooked, being left out, unfairness, loneliness, and other challenges.

My mother often reminded me of the poem by Henry Wadsworth Longfellow, in which he states, "The heights by great men [women] reached and kept were not attained by sudden flight, but they, while their companions slept, were toiling upward in the night."[53] Life is not fair, nor is it easy. Our children will be battered, bruised, broken, and defeated and get their noses bloodied, and all of that may be happening when they are alone, beyond our help or support. They must, because of the Sovereign Lord's help, get back on their feet and continue, as in Isaiah 50:7. We must pray that God will grant them the mental toughness they need to keep pressing on, not conceding defeat, staying in the game. As the writer to the Hebrews admonishes, "And let us run with perseverance the race marked out for us, fixing our eyes on Jesus" (Hebrews 12:1–2).

Conclusion and Prayer

Character is no longer regarded as a great asset by society. Situational justification is readily provided for character flaws, and there appears to be little incentive to pursue a life of good character. In the cultural context to which our children are or will be exposed, they will face challenges, and there may be no motivation to build and develop strong character. In the shifting sands of prosperity, fame, recognition, status, and pressure to accumulate wealth regardless of the means, our children will need our prayers to keep them grounded in the teaching of the Holy Scriptures while being world changers and making an impact in whatever situation our Holy God has placed them.

> Holy God, I pray that You will give _____ the desire to pursue a life of strong character evidenced by the nine traits and more all the days of his/her life. Please empower _____ to make a difference in and bring hope, meaning, and purpose to the lives of individuals he/she encounters. In times of temptation to compromise and "go with the flow," may God the Holy Spirit give him/her the necessary strength and clarity to consider the consequences and cost and then to decide on the best course of action. I pray, Lord Jesus, that You will help _____ with the increased demonstration of character traits commensurate with the situation with which he/she is faced. I pray for a deep desire in _____ to work on and build every character trait that glorifies You through both words and actions. I pray that_____ will trust You with his/her failures, weaknesses, and any potential area of compromise. Please show _____ that You have never failed anyone, nor will You fail anyone who seeks Your strength and protection. At times of disobedience and compromise, God the Holy Spirit, I pray that _____ will pay heed to Your promptings and quickly rectify his/her actions. May _____ never take Your grace or love for granted but find ways to discover the manifestation of Your goodness in everyday life. I pray this prayer in the name of Your Holy Son and our Lord Jesus Christ. Amen and amen.

Prayer Markers: Character

On this day [date]	I prayed for

On this day [date]	I prayed for

CHAPTER SIX

Calling

L EMUEL NELSON BELL WAS BORN IN LONGDALE, ALLEGHANY County, Virginia, and attended Washington and Lee University. He was an incredibly talented baseball player, and it was even speculated that he would pursue a professional career in the sport. He initially studied prelaw then changed his major to premed. Lemuel went to medical school and graduated from the Medical College of Virginia in 1916 at the age of twenty-one. Three weeks later, he married Virginia Myers Leftwich, and the two sailed for China as missionaries. Dr. Bell worked tirelessly performing up to fifteen surgeries per day while being a witness for our Lord Jesus Christ. There was a perfect blend of career and calling in these lives, not that they did not face challenges and struggles. They served in China for over twenty-five years, and their second daughter, Ruth Bell, would later marry Rev. Dr. Billy Graham.

On the other hand, we have seen Christian men and women have an enormous positive influence not only through what they did in the business world but also in the lives of those they impacted. A

Zimbabwean Christian businessman, according to Christian web site Manna Express (mannaexpressonline.com), reads his Bible for four hours on his busy days and personally sponsors the education of about twenty-two orphans in Zimbabwe. Cher Wang is cited as another example of a devoted Christian woman who leads a technology organization out of Taiwan. Of course, here in the US, we have the founders of Hobby Lobby and Chick-fil-A who have not been shy about publicly expressing their faith in our Lord Jesus Christ. Across this great land, numerous individuals are followers of our Lord Jesus Christ while accomplishing great things in their professions.

Why is this important?

A *Forbes* article (October 25, 2019) claimed that 50 percent of all American workers were unhappy with their jobs.[54] Additionally, according to an article published on December 3, 2020, by Staff Squared HR, a global Gallup poll revealed that a mere 15 percent were satisfied with what they do.[55] It has been my experience that people who are unhappy or feel that they are in the wrong line of work impact not only themselves but also the work that is entrusted to them. Studies have shown that such negativity usually results in extremely low morale and a very toxic work environment. It also affects the employee's family and social life. Imagine spending an entire working lifetime in this fashion.

On the other hand, I have met people who have secular professions yet think they should be in full-time ministry as well as those in full-time ministry who think they should be in the business world. Warren Wiersbe, in his book *So That's What a Christian Is!*, makes this point powerfully. "God has a 'lane' for each of His children to run in and a goal for each to reach." Wiersbe further points out that we all run our races to bring glory to God. We should pray that our children find the "lanes" that God has for them and that they will bring glory to God as they run that race. As I have worked with and led organizations, I have realized that it is in the identification that much of the challenge lies. If they are not able to do this, children wander in college from major to major, unclear of what they should be pursuing. Loss of time is also an important result. Only God can provide the clarity they need and sustain them in their decision.[56]

We can all wish and pray that our children will find satisfaction in their careers or fulfillment in their calling to serve the Lord Jesus Christ. When I was growing up, at every special youth gathering, there were usually two altar calls. The first was a call to accept our Lord Jesus Christ as our Savior and become His follower, and the second altar call was usually an invitation to serve Him in a full-time capacity. At one time, there were more young people who had responded to the call than there were organizations to absorb them. On the other hand, I also found people who were trying to find a compromise between what they enjoyed doing and serving God. So a hybrid version was promulgated by which if you are good at your job and you are a witness for Jesus Christ while doing that, you are serving God.

In my view, as a follower of our Lord Jesus Christ, one is expected to show skill and excellence in all that we do. In their book *Life @ Work, Marketplace Success for People of Faith*, John Maxwell, Stephen Graves, and Thomas Addington define *skill* as "understanding something completely and transforming that knowledge into creations of wonder and excellence." Elaborating further, they assert,

> The biblical definition of skill, however, goes much beyond mere knowledge, comprehensive as it may be. In addition to knowing something completely, skill also implies the capacity to translate knowledge into something of great value.[57]

The Merriam-Webster Dictionary defines *career* as "a field for or pursuit of consecutive progressive achievement especially in public, professional, or business life."[58]

Sometimes parents attempt to relive their lives through their children. Growing up, I was fascinated by martial arts and trained in a particular style of unarmed combat. I read books, trained, practiced, and wanted to qualify as a black belt, which was very difficult in those days. Unfortunately, an injury while training forced me to quit the sport altogether. When my daughter was in grade school, I convinced her to start training in martial arts as well. I quickly learned that she was doing it just to please me and was deriving no pleasure from it, although she was good at it. My intentions were good and done in the interests of my daughter, but I realized I was projecting onto her my desire to excel in pursuit.

In our overwhelming love for our children, we can sometimes get carried away into thinking we know better than God. A doctor who enjoyed being a doctor wanted her daughter to follow in her footsteps and forced her to go to medical school. The girl finished her medical degree and handed it over to her mother, saying, "This is for you. Now I will go and become an artist." I love Psalm 139:13, where David says, "For you created my inmost being, knit me together in my mother's womb." I find the word *knit* so powerful and intentional. It signifies the bringing together of many strands of a child's life in ways that only God can, in perfect alignment.

"The call" is the term that traditionally refers to God's invitation to a person to join Him in His work. God is already at work in various segments of our society, and followers of our Lord Jesus Christ are to join Him in that work. When we realize that, understand our calling, and join Him, it is one of the most fulfilling things in our lives. It is then that the purpose and place in history of every person is realized. Maxwell, Graves, and Anderson define *a calling* as "God's personal invitation for me to work on His agenda, using the talents I have been given in ways that are externally significant."[59] In agreement with this definition is the one offered by Os Guinness in his book *The Call*.

Calling is the truth that God calls us to himself so decisively that everything we are, everything we do, and everything we have is invested with a special devotion and dynamism lived out as a response to His summons and service.[60]

I propose two points for prayer on this topic.

1. Pray that children would be aware of and sensitive to the call—and obey.

If one were to follow much of the trend in the Holy Scriptures, God seems to be reaching out to individuals when they are young. It is estimated that Samuel was called by God when he was only eleven years old. Imagine the sacrifice his parents must have made when they took him to the temple and left him there to serve under a high priest. First Samuel 1:22 relates that Samuel's mother, Hannah, told her husband of her plan to present Samuel before God once he was weaned and that he would live there always. Bible scholars suggest that the age of weaning could be anywhere from three to nine. In this instance, Hannah takes the lead, and her husband supports her. First Samuel 1:23 says, "'Do what seems best to you,' Elkanah her husband told her." What a strong and courageous woman she was, and what an equally trusting and supportive husband was Elkanah!

I recall my mother telling me about a tradition in the villages of southern India, where our origins could be traced, in which the first child was always dedicated to God. Today, that part of India has the largest number of individuals serving God as full-time missionaries, evangelists, pastors, and preachers. It is also one of the most fertile and prosperous parts of the state. One example was Samuel Kamaleson. He drew his roots from that same part of southern India. He had lost his dad when he was four years of age and was raised by a single mom—her only child. She reskilled herself after she became a widow and took low-paying jobs to support herself and her son, but she had the courage and tenacity of Hannah. She relentlessly prayed that God would use Kamaleson, dedicating him to God. He was no easy son to raise; he was extremely rebellious. His mother prayed every day that God would grant him

- the devotion of Mary, Martha, Mary Magdalene, Esther, Ruth, Deborah, Job, Joseph, and Abraham
- the patience of Job
- the strength of Samson
- the gift of praise like David
- the gift of leadership like Joshua

God heard this widow's prayer. In Kamaleson's fourth year in veterinary school, he noticed a difference in the life of his roommate and asked him about it. His roommate had his roots in a different religion and told Kamaleson that he had become a follower of our Lord Jesus Christ. Through the testimony of that roommate, Kamaleson gave his heart to the Lord Jesus Christ and became His follower. Kamaleson qualified as a veterinarian, was a boxer at the university level, and had an outstanding singing voice. His voice was sought out by movie song producers and even won some contracts to sing in movies. During all that success, God tapped Kamaleson on the shoulder and invited him to work in obedience to His agenda.

Kamaleson worked under the leadership of one of his friends to start the vacation Bible school movement in India in 1952. Out of that movement arose a group of twenty-five youngsters who, during a prayer session between December 26 and 30, 1959, decided to start a group to pray for the native missionaries of India. I once had the opportunity to ask Kamaleson specifically about that occasion, and he told me it was about the time when European missionaries were leaving the country and the local news media were speculating that it may be the end of Christianity in India. It was evening as the they were praying, and as they watched the flickering lights of the city, they were suddenly overcome with a sense of burden for those who had not been introduced to the Lord Jesus Christ. Friends Missionary Prayer Band was born that night, adopting the motto "Go or Send."

Kamaleson then came to Ashbury Theological Seminary in Wilmore, Kentucky; the great of E. Stanley Jones and Bishop William Picket trained and earned graduate degrees from Ashbury and Emory universities. To make extra money during his student days, Kamaleson worked on the chicken farms of Indiana and was affectionately called "the singing veterinarian" by the farmers. Kamaleson went back to India to become a pastor all the while providing leadership to Friends Missionary Prayer Band. In 1974, he was invited by World Vision to join their evangelism pastoral leadership training team and held multiple responsibilities with that organization. Kamaleson crisscrossed the globe training pastors and evangelists, maintaining a grueling schedule. Kamaleson accepted it only on the condition that his involvement in the prayer band would not be handicapped. The prayer band grew to one of the largest missionary organizations in India, and the work continues.

One of Kamaleson's sons, Mano, went to Afghanistan as a microfinance specialist to help in rebuilding that region and was killed in a car bomb explosion. Shortly before that, Kamaleson's wife of over sixty years had died. Though heartbroken, he spoke forgiveness through the power of our Lord Jesus Christ for the people who killed his son. When the ordinary life of a seemingly ordinary child is dedicated to an extraordinary Savior, He takes it and creates an extraordinary life in that child, leaving a legacy for generations to come.

It was D. L. Moody who is reported to have said, "The world has yet to see what God can do with a man [woman] fully dedicated to Him." At the point when God extends an invitation, there must be a significant element of obedience in the response. Jonah was a classic case of disobedience and resistance (Jonah 1:3 and 4:1). When Jonah did not obey God, he lost touch with his calling and became so dissatisfied with his life that he wanted to die (Jonah 4:3). When a person is disobedient or resistant to the calling, life becomes difficult. The call never dies or goes away. It is like a flame that becomes dim—diminished but always burning. I believe there are at least three ways in which God calls His followers to join Him in His work. This is by no stretch of the imagination an exhaustive list. I do not claim to understand all the ways that the Holy God extends His invitation. These are some of the predominant ways I have seen:

The Call of Moses

This is the most direct call that an individual can receive—an audible invitation to join God and work on His agenda. The book of Exodus captures the magnitude and profoundness of this exchange in Exodus 3:4. It was a very personal call to a man who had spent forty years in the wilderness. Moses was simply going about his day when suddenly, in a very private and personal manner, God spoke to him. Imagine the emotions of a man like Moses—long forgotten by time, only relevant to the close circle of his immediate family and the sheep under his care. I have pictured that encounter many times in my mind. God, in all His tenderness and mercy, opens His heart to Moses on the suffering of the people of Israel.

God was sharing something with Moses that was breaking His heart. It was the late Bob Pierce, the founder of World Vision and Samaritan's Purse, who wrote, "Let my heart be broken with the things that break the heart of God." As the result of this prayer, Bob joined the Holy God in founding two of the most effective relief organizations in the world.

God may still call our children in an audible way today. The call may also come through the Holy Scriptures as God's irrefutable Word. Today, many followers of our Lord Jesus Christ serve the weak, marginalized, and voiceless. Sometimes we can be the answer to our prayers and frustration to what we see around us. Moses was angry at the treatment of his fellow Israelites and was willing to kill the oppressor. The Israelites, on the other hand, were frustrated that God was not hearing their prayers for deliverance.

A little girl from a small town in Indiana called Seymore was so disturbed by global sex trafficking of women that she prayed about it. As she grew up and became a young woman, God brought a wonderful man into her life who shared her burden. They worked for some years in Indiana, and then God invited them to work with Him on the rescue and education of women victimized by sex trafficking in an Asian country. They quit their jobs and, with their three children, relocated to that Asian country to serve on the front lines of the war against sex trafficking.

The Call of David

The call of David is an instance when God asks someone to communicate the invitation on His behalf. David was a shepherd. First Samuel 16 captures the powerful call and anointing of David. Samuel arrived in David's village, and there was fear among the people who misinterpreted the significance of his visit. The amazing thing is that God did not give specific details to Samuel before the actual anointing. Samuel's instructions were simple. "Go down the line of Jesse's sons, and I will show you." Jesse had not even considered David to be part of the lineup. All seven of his brothers had characteristics that would have made them ideal choices, but God rejected all of them. David had none of the characteristic of his brothers, but God saw potential in him that even his earthly father did not see. When God instructed Samuel to go to Jesse's house, he was carrying a message but for a very unlikely candidate.

Some of our children may be the most unlikely candidates, but God looks at them through a different lens altogether. It is unclear how much David, or the small group that was assembled there, understood the significance of Samuel's act, but they were in total compliance with the requirements for a sacrifice. In 1 Samuel 16:5, Samuel requires them to "consecrate themselves." *The Moody Bible Commentary* defines *consecrating* as "to set oneself apart for God." Further expounding, the commentary points out that it involved ceremonial cleansing and abstaining from some types of food and physical pleasures.[61] In other words, in this context, it was to create the right environment for the messenger and the child.

We must take every effort to expose our children to the various ways that God is served by people who have responded to His call. Timothy was a great example of one who was raised in a right environment. In 2 Timothy 1:5, Paul praises the two women who had invested in Timothy's life and provided a wonderful environment for him: his mother and grandmother. When I was growing up, a constant stream of missionaries was hosted in our modest home. I grew up listening to missionaries. When a Samuel comes along and wants to anoint our children, they must be ready.

I love the story of Deborah related in Judges 4. She was a woman who was a judge during exceedingly difficult times, and in the absence of any formal government, she settled the differences of the people who came to her. There was an opposing king called Jabin who posed a threat to her nation. Deborah, on God's instructions, sent for a man called Barak and gave him the message that God had called him to lead the army of Israel. She was the messenger, but it was a personal message to Barak. We must pray that our children will recognize the messenger, ponder the message, and obey.

The Call of Isaiah

Isaiah 6 records the call of Isaiah. It records the timing as the year King Uzziah died. The Holy Scriptures do not include a single word that has neither substance nor significance. We read about the reign of King Uzziah in 2 Kings 15 and in 2 Chronicles 26. He is referred to as Azariah in 2 Kings. He ascended to the throne when he was sixteen years of age and reigned for fifty-two years. According to the account in the 2 Chronicles, he was a military leader, innovator, builder, restorer, and hands-on agriculturist. The Holy Scriptures also give credit to King Uzziah for trying to do what pleased God. However, in the later years of his life, according to 2 Chronicles 26:16–21, he was struck with leprosy after he tried out of pride to usurp the duties of a priest. Because of his leprosy, he could no longer enter the temple, and his son Jotham assumed his leadership responsibilities. The significance, from my perspective, is that Isaiah may have had hope that God would restore not only the health of the king but also his reverence for the Holy God. Perhaps Isaiah hoped that God's work would continue under a repentant Uzziah. Isaiah may have been disappointed that this did not happen and, when Uzziah died, was in the temple worshipping and praying to the Holy God.

We see another instance in the New Testament, in Luke 24, in the well-known passage often titled "The Road to Emmaus." Here, our risen Lord Jesus Christ joins the two disciples walking on the road and talks with them. Most striking in the conversation are the words uttered by the disciples in Luke 24:21. "But we had hoped that He was the one who was going to redeem Israel." This was probably what Isaiah felt. Then the general call goes out from God in verse 8 of Isaiah 6. "Then I heard the voice of the Lord saying, 'Whom shall I send? And who will go for us?'" Isaiah, after he was cleansed, was still in the temple and heard the call go out. Sometimes the call is not specific or by name, but someone responds to that call as it is something they care deeply about.

The most potent modern-day example of this took place in the life of Dr. Ida Scudder, a missionary doctor to India from the United States. According to Wikipedia, Ida S. Scudder was one of a line of medical missionaries to India.[62] Determined not to become a doctor or medical missionary, she was invited by D. L. Moody to study theology at the Northfield Seminary in Massachusetts.

During one visit to the south of India to attend to her ailing mother, she witnessed the death of three women due to complications in childbirth and the absence of a female doctor. Due the customs prevalent at that time, these women would accept only a female doctor to attend them. As a result, Ida Scudder became keenly aware of the need around her. The need was very great, and she felt she had seen the heart of God in the pain and misery of those women. Inspired to respond to the need, she returned to the US and enrolled in the first class of women students in Cornell Medical School, graduating in 1899. She returned to India and began to work among the women. She never married, committed her life to the mission field, and established one of the largest teaching and multispecialty hospitals in Vellore, India. This institution still carries on her work today, healing the poorest of the poor and the sick from different parts of the world.

2. Pray that they would sustain the calling.

I have always had mixed feelings about the life of King Saul. He had so much potential and all the opportunity to change the course of history. Sadly, he failed. The Holy Scriptures in 1 Samuel 9 describe the course of events that led to the anointing of Saul to be Israel's first king (1 Samuel 10:1). His pedigree demonstrated that he was pure, affluent, and physically attractive. His character included a strong work ethic in being persistent at what was assigned to him, a caring attitude toward his family, including his father, and a humble spirit in that he listened to advice.

As I read about the beginning of the fall of Saul, a few things stand out that we should pray against for our children as they serve God in their area of calling.

- *Overconfidence.* In 1 Samuel 11, the Holy Scriptures describe the military leadership of Saul. He decimated the

---

Ammonites, but afterward, he became more dependent on his own abilities than on God. For a calling to be effective, there needs to be a constant dependence on God.

- *Misplaced eagerness.* Saul overstepped the boundaries of his calling. It was not his place to offer the burnt and the fellowship offering; it was Samuel's (1 Samuel 13:9–11). When God calls an individual, he equips the individual for that calling. The equipping process includes the fine-tuning of a person's human qualities. Unless there is a leading from God followed by the equipping, the individual must not attempt to expand the scope of the calling. I have observed that any premature assumption of expansion of the calling and acting on it results in frustration and failure, the ramifications of which are hard to reverse.

- *Manipulation and dishonesty.* First Samuel 15:13–15 records the gravity of the confrontation between Samuel and Saul. Notice in 1 Samuel 15:13 that Saul states in confidence that he has carried out the instructions of God, which was not true. Also in 1 Samuel 15:13, we observe the manipulation rolling right along. Saul argued that he had disobeyed by saving the best animals so that they could be sacrificed back to God. Once manipulation and dishonesty set in, there is no stopping them. It is like a person who sleeps through a wake-up alarm. The first time is difficult, but as the person grows accustomed to it, it will not even bother them.

In a message on Mark 12:38–42, Rev. Dr. Samuel T. Kamaleson pointed to our Lord Jesus Christ speaking about professionalism in religion. I would like to extend that concept to the calling as well. It has been my experience that the longer we pursue our calling in alignment with God, the more dependent on Him we grow. We should be praying that, as our children pursue their calling, they will grow more dependent on God. While they exhibit a high level of professional competence in their calling, they must never stop depending on God every single day of their lives. The professionalism that Rev. Dr. Samuel Kamaleson addressed evidenced itself in the following areas:

- Pride. I once arranged a meeting with a popular pastor as the main speaker. Despite my best efforts, the size of the audience was not satisfactory to him, and he made no bones about it.
- Demand for respect and recognition.
- Hunger for power; greed. This describes one who would even demand the best seats at a gathering and ask to be served at the cost of others. Our Lord Jesus Christ in Mark pivots to address the attitude of the teachers of the Law toward treatment of the weak and voiceless like widows.

I was once at the clinic of a popular orthopedic surgeon, a professing Christian, in an Asian country. While he stepped out of his office to welcome me, he noticed that there was a lady also waiting there. From her attire, it appeared that she was a person of no great means. The doctor loudly announced to his front office staff that he was treating her for free and that she could wait.

I can never reiterate enough how important it is for the calling of our children to stay fresh every single day of their lives, that they will place the interests of the One who has called them above their own, and that they will credit all their successes to the One who invited them in the first place.

Conclusion and Prayer

Discovering their calling, the purpose of their existence, and fulfilling that calling will create immense satisfaction and significance in the lives of our children. How satisfying it will be when success is not the main pursuit of their lives. We must pray that the Holy God will grant them the skills, training, and experience to keep them progressing. It is also important that they be surrounded with a support system, such as mentors, coaches, and peers. Above all, it is important that our children recognize the call and obey it. Once they recognize the call and pursue the Holy God in obedience, He will use them for the glory of His name and for the extension of His kingdom.

Holy God, I pray that You will make the calling for _____ truly clear and give him/her the strength and confidence to follow You in that calling. I pray that _____ will realize that he/she can live with joy and purpose if only he/she trusts You. God the Holy Spirit, I pray that You will refresh and renew his/her spirit every day and help him/her to balance his/her life as _____ juggles various priorities. Please equip _____ for Your calling all through his/her life. Please provide _____ with the necessary support in his/her calling commensurate with the challenges that he/she faces or will face. In moments of anxiety, doubt, or temporary failure, please reassure and support _____ through Your Word directly or indirectly. When _____ feels like giving up or walking away, please remind him/her that You never make mistakes and every challenge that he/she faces can only make him/her stronger. I pray for focus on the calling throughout his/her life till You redirect or reassign. I pray for Your protection, peace, provision, and power as _____ follows Your calling. May all who meet _____ be blessed by his/her expertise. I pray this prayer in the name of Your Holy Son and our Lord Jesus Christ. Amen and amen.

Prayer Markers: Calling

On this day [date]	I prayed for

On this day [date]	I prayed for

Country

I HAD NOT ORIGINALLY PLANNED FOR THIS *C*. IT WAS AN afterthought after the long-lasting ravages of the events of the year 2020. Amid a crippling pandemic, our grandson was born prematurely by about a month. Etched in my mind is the night our son-in-law called and said our daughter had gone into labor. As my wife and I drove to Tennessee, it occurred to me that a new life was given by God during very trying and difficult circumstances. It occurred to me that I needed to be more deliberate and focused on praying for the country in which he and the generations to follow will live. What kind of country do we want that to be?

Praying for the country is one of the most intense forms of defense against spiritual warfare. It requires committed and deliberate prayer warriors. We have a choice to make. Either we can complain and be indifferent to the kind of country the generations to come will inhabit or we can be focused and deliberate in our intercession, fully aware that the "God whose eyes watch the nations" (Psalm 66:7) will hear our prayer and carry out His means of damage control.

As a young believer, I was so fascinated by the revivals or awakenings that took place all over the world since the death and resurrection of our Lord Jesus Christ. I imagined what it would be like to be part of a revival. I heard stories and read books on the Korean, Ugandan, and Indonesian revivals—how they were outpourings of God the Holy Spirit rivaled only by the first Pentecost. I have also read about the Azusa Street revival, the Asbury revival, the Pensacola revival, and the Irish revival. Recently I heard testimonies of what is happening in Iran where God is meeting and healing lives so much so that all established and approved forms of Christianity have been caught off guard. I believe that never in the history of humanity has there been a direct revelation of our Lord Jesus Christ to those who seek Him as we are seeing now. What is exciting to me is much of the action is happening not in established forms of Christianity but in a tender, direct meeting of the Savior with those who seek to be saved. The revelation is direct, and the message personal. It is my prayer that the people of every nation will experience the revelation of our Lord Jesus Christ in a way that has not been experienced before. I am also of the view that no nation in the world has experienced head-on the transformational force of the Triune God as did some of the biblical nations like Nineveh.

We are so satisfied with meager rustling instead of praying for a gale force encounter. I am not in any way belittling the work that God is doing in transforming lives, but we as followers of our Lord Jesus Christ should be praying for a revival that engulfs the whole nation starting with the church. God can do much more, and we ain't seen nothing yet.

In James 4:3, we read, "When you ask, you do not receive, because you ask with wrong motives." I have been part of prayer meetings where prayers have been made to bless a method, speaker, or performer and in turn bring about a revival. If any nation needs to experience a revival of the kind we have not seen before, there needs to be a simple, unadulterated proclamation of the gospel of our Lord Jesus Christ—not methods, not programs, not charismatic preachers, and not performers. In the proclamation of the gospel, everything needs to point to the Holy Triune God, the work of His beloved Son on Calvary, and the transformation He can bring about in each individual life.

I would argue that there were, are, and will be better preachers than Rev. Dr. Billy Graham, but his simple, unwavering proclamation of the gospel was what generated the response that we saw at his meetings. I was a volunteer at his crusades in India, and one of my assignments was to secure a rope line close to where he passed on his way to the podium. As I watched him pass me night after night, dressed in a modest suit and tie, carrying his well-worn Bible, I realized that he was an ordinary man who was laser focused on proclaiming in simple terms the extraordinary message of the gospel. Every minute he spent on that podium was spent focusing on the message of our Lord Jesus Christ and nothing else. His mission was urgent and critical, and it appeared to me that he was fully aware that he would never see again or personally meet most of the people in the audience.

Rev. Dr. Billy Graham gave a simple, straightforward message that was translated into two languages followed by an invitation accompanied by the choir singing the immortal hymn "Just as I Am." To this the response was extraordinary. They came poor, rich, with different skin colors, city folk, country folk, all age groups, educated, and illiterate. *That* is the power of the gospel.

I was recently listening to an interview with Billy Graham's song leader, Cliff Barrows, who was reminiscing about a crusade that was held in the UK. The press on seeing the response had concluded that it was the emotion attached to the song "Just as I Am" that was generating the enormous response. Dr. Graham was worried that the focus was shifting and requested that Barrows provide no singing or music when he gave the invitation. Barrows recalled that, for the thirty nights of that series of meetings, there was no music or singing at the time of the invitation, but the response never diminished. Such is the transforming power of the gospel!

Nehemiah is one of my favorite characters in the Holy Scriptures. Even though he had a comfortable life as a cupbearer to a king, he had a burden for Jerusalem. Not only that, but it was also a burden that he translated into action. Picking up in Nehemiah 1, we read that he first sought accurate information.

Too many of us are indifferent to the happenings in our own country. I have heard many people tell me such things as "I've stopped reading the newspaper or listening to the news as it's too depressing." In my view, that is exactly why we should be aware of what is going on in our country and pray for God's intervention.

I am reminded of Ezekiel 22:30. "I looked for a man [woman] among them who would build up the wall and stand before me in the gap on behalf of the land so I would not have to destroy it, but I found no one." As someone once said, we as followers of our Lord Jesus Christ should be taking the needs of our country on one hand, the eternal promises of the Holy God on the other, and pray for the country. That is what I believe it means to stand in the gap. The biggest misfortune among followers of our Lord Jesus Christ is indifference to the condition of our countries.

The next thing Nehemiah did with the information was to weep, mourn, fast, and pray (Nehemiah 1:4). Sometimes, even when we have the information, we complain and truly do little. Every country needs informed people who will stand in the gap for their nation—people who will weep, mourn, fast, and pray for their nation. If we want our children to have better lives after us, it is incumbent on us to weep, mourn, fast, and pray for our nation, including certain groups and issues.

Political Leaders of the Country

The Holy Scriptures command us to pray for our leaders. In 1 Timothy 2:1–2, Paul writes,

> I urge, then, first of all, that requests, prayers, intercession, and thanksgiving be made for

everyone—for kings and all those in authority, that
we may live peaceful and quiet lives in all godliness
and holiness.

So why is it important to pray for the political leadership? Most
importantly, they make decisions on war and peace in addition
to the peaceful and quiet existence of our children. But history is
replete with leaders who are corrupt, who circumvent the law and the
founding documents, who manipulate, mislead, cheat, steal, stamp
out any differing views, and above all, are more concerned about
their own well-being than the welfare of the people they govern.

The Holy Scriptures are no stranger to corrupt political leaders.
In fact, in the book of Genesis, chapter 34, we are told about a ruler
who violates the dignity of a woman to whom he was attracted. Our
Lord Jesus Christ crossed paths with corrupt politicians right from
his birth to his death and resurrection. Herod lied to the wisemen
at the time of our Lord's birth (Matthew 2:8). An immoral Herod
beheaded John the Baptist because John did not condone Herod's
immorality (Matthew 14:3–12). Keep in mind that John the Baptist
was the cousin of our Lord Jesus Christ, and one can safely assume
that they had a close relationship. Matthew 14:13 records, "When
Jesus heard what had happened [the execution of John the Baptist],
he withdrew by boat privately to a solitary place."

The political institution used bribery to have Judas betray our
Lord Jesus Christ. (Matthew 26:14–16) The final trial was a sham,
and in a gross miscarriage of justice, false witnesses were used to
ensure the release of a criminal, Barabbas, and the conviction of
the innocent Savior. Even after Christ's death and resurrection, the
religious elite, in cahoots with the politicians, bribed the guards
and circulated misinformation. Our Lord Jesus Christ held back
no punches and called Herod a fox in Luke 13:32. This by most
accounts was an insult.

The unfortunate consequence of compromised political
leadership is the suffering of regular citizens with violence, injustice,
and denied opportunities. While King David himself was no shining

example, Psalm 56, which is attributed to him, gives some insight on our prayers for political leaders. Of course, while praying for guidance and wisdom, this psalm also reminds us in verse 7 that God is powerful enough to bring down nations. We should pray our political leaders have this realization. Psalm 58 is another psalm that is attributed to King David and addresses corrupt political leadership. Expounding on this psalm, the *Today in the Word* monthly devotional of Moody Bible Institute points out that verse 1—"Do you rulers indeed speak justly? Do you judge uprightly among men?"—could be best understood as "corrupt human rulers, who were encouraged and empowered by malevolent spiritual entities."[63]

The seeking of the spiritual entities by political leaders is not a new concept in the Holy Scriptures. King Saul sought the advice of mediums, and the Holy Scriptures also talk about Queen Jezebel, through her allegiance to the Baals, slaughtered the prophets and persecuted the prophet Elijah (1 Kings 18–19). As a countermeasure to this kind of unholy alliance, King David prays to God using very graphic descriptions. But in essence, as the Moody Bible Institute's exposition on this psalm postulates, "David prays that these rulers would become powerless to continue their oppression."[64]

Justice System and Law Enforcement

My father was a police officer and a follower of our Lord Jesus Christ. He was not ashamed about his faith, and it was public knowledge that he was a Christian, but, even as a little boy, I was so amazed at the trust and confidence that people from different worldviews or religions had in him. His jurisdiction included different places of worship, and a vast majority of them were not Christian, yet he made sure that their safety was assured and that the devotees could gather for worship peacefully.

I had the privilege of visiting other faith leaders with him, and when the leaders of other faiths wanted to bless me as a little boy, my father respectfully agreed and I was the recipient of those wishes and blessings. I thank God for the legacy and influence my father left behind. I was only six years old when he passed away, but those were six impactful years that I will never forget. We need to pray that every law enforcement officer will uphold the law without partiality or prejudice. It does not take an entire lifetime for a dad to influence his children; it only takes time well spent and a real-life demonstration of his faith and values.

I have a childhood friend who qualified as an attorney and cleared the civil services exam to become a powerful bureaucrat. He felt led to pursue a career as an attorney and built a successful practice. One day, God directed his attention to what could be called the "forgotten prisoners"—those who were too poor to afford credible legal representation, whose documentation fell through the cracks, or who were simply forgotten but continued to be incarcerated. Some of these individuals were a distant memory to their families. He started a ministry to identify and provide legal representation to those forgotten individuals. Those who were released were reunited with their families or what was left of them. He was selected to be a judge at the highest court in the state but turned it down to continue his work among the forgotten.

The Holy Scriptures in Isaiah 1:17 clearly direct, "Learn to do right! Seek justice. Encourage the oppressed. Defend the cause of the fatherless; plead he case of the widow." In Micah 6:8, the Holy Scriptures plainly instruct, "And what does the Lord require of you? To act justly and to love mercy and to walk humbly before your God." Leviticus 19:15 absolutely nails it. "Do not pervert justice; do not show partiality to the poor or favoritism to the great, but judge your neighbor fairly." Deuteronomy 16:19–20 warns, "Do not pervert justice or show partiality. Do not accept a bribe, for a bribe blinds the eyes of the wise and twists the words of the righteous."

I have had the opportunity to travel to quite a few countries worldwide and have seen God's accusation in Isaiah 10:1–2 play out.

> Woe to those who make unjust laws, to those who
> issue oppressive decrees, to deprive the poor of their
> rights and withhold justice from the oppressed of
> my people, making widows their prey and robbing
> the fatherless.

I would also add one more category of people who suffer most under a compromised judiciary: the elderly. It is a frightening and terrifying experience. I was once in a country that practices such and by mistake had left my travel papers, including my local contact information, at my hotel. I quickly realized how vulnerable I was. God takes the injustice that is meted out to his children very seriously and asks in Isaiah 10:3, "What will you do on the day of reckoning, when disaster comes from afar? To whom will you run for help? Where will you leave your riches?" We must pray that every time our children avail the services of law enforcement or must access the judicial system for remedies, they will be treated fairly and expeditiously. Of course, we must pray for every component of the judiciary and law enforcement that it will not be corrupted or compromised in the first place.

Borders of the Country and Those Who Defend the Land

I am fully aware that, here in the United States, the very word *borders* evokes different points of view. Whether we like it or not, borders are a reality from the beginning of time; good as well as bad things can come across them. I heard a Bible scholar explain that during biblical times, even the gods were territorial; it was believed that when you crossed into the territory of another god, one needed to pay homage to that god. That is why, when Jonah was asked to go to Nineveh and he fled toward Tarshish, he felt he was getting away from the reach and influence of God, who was believed to have been based in Jerusalem.

137

One of the earliest references to borders is found in Genesis 12:11, which states, "As he [Abram] was about to enter Egypt." One can assume that there was either a marked border that he was crossing or border check post that he was approaching. In some countries, the most lethal form of drugs, human trafficking, is brought across a border that is porous or unguarded. In some cases, terrorists have snuck across the border to attack the inhabitants of that country.

We should be praying for the security of the borders of the country in which our children live. A country that does not safeguard its borders will not be able to provide dignified refuge for those who seek shelter from persecution, nor will it be able to defend them from their pursuers. Isaiah 60:18 says, "No longer will violence be heard in your land, nor ruin or destruction within your borders, but you will call your walls Salvation and your gates Praise." Without going into the prophetical technicalities, this should be the prayer of every parent or sponsor for the countries that our children will be living in.

What an amazing situation it would be when our children live in a land where violence does not even exist. Our flags are directed to be flown at half-mast every time there is an incident that involves substantial loss of life. The sad fact is the flags seem to be at half-mast most of the time. Understandably, this is a fallen world, but that does not give us an excuse to neglect praying for the peace and the absence of violence. The prophet Isaiah also talks about ruin and destruction not being within the borders. Every year, countless lives are lost to multiple types of ruin and destruction and new drugs are created and introduced to addict children. What is advocated today becomes harmful tomorrow as children are exposed to new types of addictions.

When I was in school, we read a well-known poem written in 1854 by Alfred, Lord Tennyson, called "The Charge of the Light Brigade." It was a depiction of the heroism of six hundred soldiers who rode into a barrage of cannon and gun fire. Very few survived. The poet based his content on the Crimean War and the casualties suffered by the Light Cavalry Brigade in the Battle of Baclava. Even as a little boy, while I was amazed at the courage of those six hundred men, I was disturbed by one line in the poem. "Not tho' the soldier knew/Someone had blunder'd." Obviously, someone had made a mistake by sending these men into battle. The question haunted me: how could anyone take such a decision so lightly and not invest into it enough due diligence?

In his book *A Table in the Presence*, Lt. Carey H. Cash, a chaplain who served with the US Marines, captures the emotion surrounding the death of men and women on the battlefield.[65] We must pray that every leader takes seriously the responsibility of making decisions that put men and women in harm's way. Committees and commissions can be installed, or blame assigned, but not one lost life can be restored. Every father, mother, wife, husband, son, or daughter lost can never be replaced or substituted.

In 2 Samuel 11:14, King David sent an innocent man, Uriah, into battle with the wrong motivation. The man was killed, and David got into permanent trouble. The Holy God did not take this action lightly. He held King David accountable, and some of the consequences were perpetual. It can be argued that this was the outcome of David's adultery, which is true. But the prophet Nathan in 2 Samuel 12:9 refers to the sword as the means that King David himself used to take Uriah's life. God, through Nathan, also pronounces the terminal consequences when in 2 Samuel 12:10 he proclaims, "Now therefore, the sword will never depart from your house."

Educational Institutions and Seminaries

Paul, who was arguably one of the most educated followers of our Lord Jesus Christ, was called mad in Acts 26:24. Paul was making his defense before Festus when Festus shouted, "Your great learning is driving you insane." On the other hand, in John 7:15, on listening to the teaching of Jesus, "the Jews were amazed and asked, 'How did this man get such learning without having studied?'"

As I write this book, I cannot overemphasize the need for prayer for our educational institutions, both public and private. It is no longer a question of whether they instill Christian values or not but whether institutions will simply teach the truth without distortion, manipulation, or political bias. Many institutions that were founded as Christian institutions are Christian in name only today, and some of them have changed so much that they have become unrecognizable in content and character. Not every parent will have the luxury of sending their kids to the few truly Christian institutions that still exist.

Educational institutions, and their teachers, wield enormous power in deciding the mindset of future professionals in every sphere of human existence. It has been my experience that, in the marketplace of knowledge, the loudest and most often repeated arguments are quickly acknowledged as truth. It is our duty to pray that educational institutions will provide education truthfully to our children, without bias or prejudice, and allow our children to draw their own inferences. Our children must be able to pull the various strings of education they receive in the context of the moral framework provided by the God of the Holy Scriptures.

Nature and the Environment

There seems to be a common perception among some Christians that the Holy God has placed nature and environment at the disposal of human beings to use and abuse as they please. My reading of the Holy Scriptures places us in a position of stewardship, and we have a responsibility to take care of nature.

In my travels, I have been amazed at the work of God in various nations of the world from the most arid to the most fertile. In Psalm 19:1, King David says, "The heavens declare the glory of God; the skies proclaim the work of His hands." My wife and my brother-in-law are avid stargazers, and picking up on their conversations, I started to get interested in some concepts about the stars and galaxies. I have been amazed and dumbfounded. What an awesome God we serve! My mother was an avid gardener and tree planter. People around us consulted her on the type of trees they should plant and the types of plants they could afford.

Nature is the incredible handiwork of the Holy God. John 1:3 presents a powerful declaration. "Through Him all things were made; and without Him nothing was made that has life." Job, in one of his meaningful responses to his friends in Job 12:7–10, says,

> But ask the animals, and they will teach you, or the birds of the air, and they will tell you; or speak to the earth, and it will teach you, or let the fish of the sea inform you. Which of all these does not know that the hand of the Lord has done this?

We have a responsibility as followers of our Lord Jesus Christ to do everything possible to leave the environment for future generations to enjoy. I am not talking about activism but a plain, common sense approach in gratitude to the Holy God who created it and allows us to enjoy it. In Psalm 65:9–13, the psalmist gives us an indication of what we should be praying for.

> You care for the land and water it; You enrich it abundantly. The streams of God are filled with water to provide the people with grain, for so You have ordained it. You drench its furrows and level its ridges; You soften it with showers and bless its crops. You crown the year with Your bounty, and Your carts overflow with abundance. The grasslands of the dessert overflow; the hills are clothed with gladness. The meadows are covered with flocks and the valleys are mantled with grain; they shout for joy and sing.

It is His creation. We are only passing through, and we have a responsibility to seek His blessing as we experience it in all its fullness and majesty.

Churches and Christian Leaders

Churches and Christian leaders in every country need our prayer. It is a matter of great disappointment to see the rising divisions in the church and among churches. In John 17, our Lord Jesus Christ, just before His death and resurrection, prays a powerful prayer addressed to the Holy Father. In verse 11, He prays, "I will remain in the world no longer, but they are still in the world, and I am coming to You. Holy Father, protect them by the power of Your name—the name You gave me—so that they may be one as we are one." What a powerful and relevant prayer!

One of the most important reasons why churches lose sight of their mission is bureaucracy, the resulting dysfunction, and sometimes even internal corruption. Usually bureaucracy creeps in under the guise of improving systems resulting in setting up of structures, forms to be filled out in person or online, appointments to be made, and complexity introduced in mission, ministry, and technology.

The acid test for bureaucracy is how quickly the poor, weak, and marginalized in the church and outside can get help. Bureaucracy increases the selection process and the lead time to provide help. On the other hand, a church that is passionate in being an instrument of our Lord Jesus Christ will find ways to take help to those in need and reduce bureaucracy. I am a firm believer that efficiency of a ministry is determined by the time taken from the time a request for help is made or identifies to the time the help is actually provided. Efficient churches will always try to reduce this timeline and not increase it.

I knew of a church that had a passion to help those who had mental illness. A counselor was engaged, and people could walk in and get help in times of need. Over time, the counselor decided to grow the ministry. Other counselors were hired, office buildings were procured, glass offices were built, a receptionist was positioned, partnerships with corporations and institutions were established, an appointment software was rolled out, and on and on. The result was that those who could walk in and get help now needed to first go online, make an appointment, and wait for their appointment time to meet with people who sat in glass offices.

To our Lord Jesus Christ, it was all about the people who needed help, and the more complexity and bureaucracy churches introduce, the farther they get from those they intend to serve. We must pray that the churches in this country never lose sight of the mission and purpose for their existence.

Conclusion and Prayer

I cannot in any way overemphasize the importance of praying for the country in which our children will live. Among the many things the COVID-19 pandemic exposed in most nations worldwide is the absence of leadership with foresight. Many died, and many more suffered from inept services handicapped by corruption, apathy, and negligence. Political battles were fought, statistics were doctored, aid was mishandled, and the media took sides promoting a narrative that was supportive of one side of the political spectrum over another, even pushing false information. The poor, weak, and marginalized were the most impacted. The world felt the need for leaders who could rise above concern for their own political future and place the interests of the peoples of their nations above personal political survival.

Holy God, I pray for the country in which
_____ will live. I pray for freedom,
protection of life, and peace in the land that
You have appointed as _____'s home
country. Whenever his/her land is threatened by

famine, pestilence, natural calamities, drought, or any threat internal or external, I pray that _____ will turn to You for refuge and pray on behalf of the people. I pray that every work of Satan and his demonic forces be neutralized and destroyed through the blood of our Lord Jesus Christ. I pray that every branch of the government and private sector will function as intended without prejudice or partiality. I pray for the educational institutions that _____ will encounter, that they will impart truthful, unbiased knowledge without any indoctrination or hidden agendas. I pray for the churches in the land, that they will always seek to do what pleases You and be Your instruments in the land. I pray for the Christian leadership in the land, that they will walk closely with You and not be a stumbling block to any who seek You. May _____ join You in Your work, Lord Jesus, and may Your name alone be glorified. I pray in the name of Your Holy Son and our Lord Jesus Christ. Amen and amen.

Prayer Markers: Country

On this day [date]	I prayed for

On this day [date]	I prayed for

John Rajanayakam

On this day [date]	I prayed for

CONCLUSION

For Generations to Come

We cannot foresee the future, but all indications are that a follower of our Lord Jesus Christ will only face challenging circumstances in a scary, polarizing world. Should the Lord tarry, Satan and his minions will intensify their efforts to unleash havoc on the lives of children. In conclusion, I want to refer to the advice that Paul gave young Timothy in his epistles: 1 and 2 Timothy. This is also my prayer for every child who decides to follow our Lord Jesus Christ, to live for Him.

In 1 Timothy 1:1–2, Paul acknowledges the spiritual influence that Timothy's mother and grandmother had on him. It is my prayer that every family will make an investment in the lives of the children entrusted to them that will have an impact for generations to come. One of the biggest legacies an individual can leave behind is the knowledge that they have done everything possible to enable future generations to follow our Lord Jesus Christ.

In Proverbs 1:8, we read, "Listen, my son to your father's instructions and do not forsake your mother's teaching." It is evident that there is an expectation from the Holy Scriptures that the father will provide instruction and the mother teaching. Of course, in our context, sponsors do have a responsibility too. No amount of wealth, possessions, comfort, or provision made by us as human beings out of love for our children will compensate for spiritual instruction and teaching. We will never know all there is to know about raising children in and of ourselves, and that is why it is so important to seek the help and intervention of the Holy God in this process. The legacy that we leave behind will not be reflected by the cars we drove, the houses we lived in, the meetings we attended, or the money we made but by the spiritual investment we made in the lives of our children.

Timothy's mother and grandmother are mentioned but a couple of times in the Holy Scriptures, but think of the legacy they left behind in the life of this young Christian. What type of legacy will you leave behind for your children?

When we finish our race here on this earth and take leave of all our earthly assignments, what a joy it will be to know that we have passed on the torch of faith to the next generation. Paul's advice to Timothy holds good even today, and I hope and pray that every child will run the race of life as the writer of Hebrews proclaims in Hebrews 12:1–2.

> Therefore, since we are surrounded by such a great cloud of witnesses, let us throw off everything that hinders and the sin that so easily entangles us, and let us run with perseverance the race marked out for us. Let us fix our eyes on Jesus, the author and perfecter of our faith.

As I see it, everything against which Paul cautions Timothy will be faced by our children as they seek to persevere in their lifelong dedication to our Lord Jesus Christ. Not the least of these will be false teachers, leadership failure, dissension within the church, distortion of the gospel, philosophies that dilute the message and mission of our Lord Jesus Christ, and a culture that grows increasingly hostile in its demands for conformity.

In Acts 20:29–30, as part of his farewell address to the Ephesian elders, Paul writes,

> I know that after I leave, savage wolves will come after you and will not spare the flock. Even from

your own number men [women] will arise and distort the truth in order to draw away disciples after them.

But amid all the hopeless and confusing circumstances, we can be assured in the words of psalmist in Psalm 77:14 when he reminds us that our Holy God is One who performs miracles.

Finally, I want to encourage you that no matter how far astray or messed up the child you are praying for seems at a point in time, persist in prayer, for the Holy God has promised that He will answer our prayers. He will perform miracles in the life of the child you are praying for beyond your wildest expectations.

I want to join you now in prayer praying over your child, _____ (fill in the name).

According to 1 Timothy 6:6–11, _____ will pursue righteousness, godliness, faith, love, endurance, and gentleness. _____ will fight the good fight, taking hold of the eternal life offered to him/her.

According to Romans 12:12, _____ will be joyful in hope, patient in affliction, and faithful in prayer.

According to 2 Timothy 1:6–14, _____ will not be ashamed of the gospel and its life-changing power in his/her life but will be aware that he/she has been entrusted with the teaching of the gospel.

May the Holy God in His mercy and grace grant that _____ and all the subsequent generations to follow him/her remain steadfast in their commitment to the gospel and our Lord Jesus Christ until He either calls them home or they see Him face-to-face.

Amen and amen.

LITANY FOR CHILDREN

This is a group prayer that can be prayed for the child either by the family or a group. The traditional way in which such liturgical prayers are prayed is a leader reads aloud the prayer in bold letters and everyone in the group or congregation follows by reading aloud the response in italics.

In the name of the Holy Father, Holy Son, and the Holy Spirit,

For a longing in _____ [child's name] to experience the transformation provided through the death and resurrection of our Lord Jesus Christ.

Holy Christ Jesus, Son of the Holy and Living God, have mercy on us, hear our prayer, love, forgive, and save _____ [child's name].

For an unquenchable thirst to be near to and know more about our Lord Jesus Christ every day of _____'s life.

God the Holy Spirit, have mercy on us, and show him/her new ways, new depths, and new experiences each day.

For safety from all harm, violence, sickness, both mental and physical, disease, danger, enemies, natural elements, that no weapon formed or any voice raised against shall prosper.

Holy Father, have mercy on us, and heal, protect, and preserve
_____. *May Your angelic protection watch over him/ her every day.*

For protection against all satanic forces, powers of darkness, evil influences, and any evil action operational now and in the future.

Holy Lord Jesus, have mercy on us and provide _____ *the power and protection of Your precious blood.*

For wisdom and strength to make choices that are pleasing to You, Holy God, and to follow through on them.

God the Holy Spirit, have mercy on us, and provide guidance, direction, determination, and self-control to _____ *in following Your leading.*

For character traits that are rooted in a relationship with our Lord Jesus Christ, for the growth and development of those traits.

Holy Lord Jesus, have mercy on us, be with _____ *, and grant him/her strength to set boundaries, resist ungodliness and worldly passions, and live a life that glorifies You.*

For help, miraculous intervention, comfort, support, peace, and enduring faith in all the challenges that _____ **will face, no matter how insurmountable they seem.**

Holy God, have mercy on us, and be with _____ *in the midst of every challenge and suffering and reveal Your powerful presence every step of the way.*

For companions who will enrich _____ 's life and for protection from those who will have a negative impact. For the orchestration of a life partner at the appointed time.

Holy God, have mercy on us, and provide _____ with the right companions all the days of his/her life, and be merciful on the marriage of _____ and his/her life partner.

For listening to Your call, discovering of life's purpose, and growing in dependence on You while _____ fulfills that calling and purpose.

Holy God, have mercy on us, and refresh _____ every day of his/her life as he/she pursues Your calling. May _____ bless all those who come into contact with his/her service. May he/she join You in Your mission here on earth.

For a life of freedom, safety, and social systems that work for the good of everyone in the country that You have chosen for _____ as his/her home, where the poor, elderly, orphans, widows, and those marginalized are not forgotten.

Holy God, have mercy on us, protect the land and all who dwell in it, bless this country, and may it be a blessing to other nations around the world.

Almighty and Merciful God, we pray that _____ will live a life of faith, believing in Your everlasting promises, and will have the assurance of an everlasting life all the days of his/her life.

We pray this in and through the name of our Lord Jesus Christ. Amen and amen.

SCRIPTURE MEMORIZATION FROM THE PSALMS

36 Months
Version: International Children's Bible

MONTH 1
Psalm 19:1–3
¹The heavens tell the glory of God.
And the skies announce what his hands have made.
²Day after day they tell the story.
Night after night they tell it again.
³They have no speech or words.
They don't make any sound to be heard.

MONTH 2
Psalm 18:30–32
³⁰The ways of God are without fault.
The Lord's words are pure.
He is a shield to those who trust him.
³¹Who is God? Only the Lord.
Who is the Rock? Only our God.
³²God is my protection.
He makes my way free from fault.

MONTH 3
Psalm 34:1–3

[1]I will praise the Lord at all times.
His praise is always on my lips.
[2]My whole being praises the Lord.
The poor will hear and be glad.
[3]Tell the greatness of the Lord with me.
Let us praise his name together.

MONTH 4
Psalm 23:1–3

[1]The Lord is my shepherd.
I have everything I need.
[2]He gives me rest in green pastures.
He leads me to calm water.
[3]He gives me new strength.
For the good of his name,
he leads me on paths that are right.

MONTH 5
Psalm 25:3–6

[4]Lord, tell me your ways.
Show me how to live.
[5]Guide me in your truth.
Teach me, my God, my Savior.
I trust you all day long.
[6]Lord, remember your mercy and love.
You have shown them since long ago.

MONTH 6
Psalm 8:3–5
³I look at the heavens,
which you made with your hands.
I see the moon and stars,
which you created.
⁴But why is man important to you?
Why do you take care of human beings?
⁵You made man a little lower than the angels.
And you crowned him with glory and honor.

MONTH 7
Psalm 18:1–3
¹I love you, Lord. You are my strength.
²The Lord is my rock, my protection, my Savior.
My God is my rock.
I can run to him for safety.
He is my shield and my saving strength, my high tower.
³I will call to the Lord.
He is worthy of praise.
And I will be saved from my enemies.

MONTH 8
Psalm 16:5–7

[5]No, the Lord is all I need.
He takes care of me.
[6]My share in life has been pleasant.
My part has been beautiful.
[7]I praise the Lord because he guides me.
Even at night, I feel his leading.

MONTH 9
Psalm 29:1–3

[1]Praise the Lord, you angels.
Praise the Lord's glory and power.
[2]Praise the Lord for the glory of his name.
Worship the Lord because he is holy.
[3]The Lord's voice is heard over the sea.
The glorious God thunders.
The Lord thunders over the great ocean.

MONTH 10
Psalm 33:4–6

[4]God's word is true.
Everything he does is right.
[5]He loves what is right and fair.
The Lord's love fills the earth.
[6]The sky was made at the Lord's command.
By the breath from his mouth, he made all the stars.

MONTH 11
Psalm 33:12–14
[12]Happy is the nation whose God is the Lord.
Happy are the people he chose for his very own.
[13]The Lord looks down from heaven.
He sees every person.
[14]From his throne he watches
everyone who lives on earth.

MONTH 12
Psalm 23:4–6
[4]Even if I walk
through a very dark valley,
I will not be afraid
because you are with me.
Your rod and your shepherd's staff comfort me.
[5]You prepare a meal for me
in front of my enemies.
You pour oil of blessing on my head.
You give me more than I can hold.
[6]Surely your goodness and love will be with me
all my life.
And I will live in the house of the Lord forever.

MONTH 13
Psalm 36:5–7

[5]Lord, your love reaches to the heavens.
Your loyalty goes to the skies.
[6]Your goodness is as high as the mountains.
Your justice is as deep as the great ocean.
Lord, you protect both men and animals.
[7]God, your love is so precious!
You protect people as a bird protects
her young under her wings.

MONTH 14
Psalm 37:5–7

[5]Depend on the Lord.
Trust him, and he will take care of you.
[6]Then your goodness will shine like the sun.
Your fairness will shine like the noonday sun.
[7]Wait and trust the Lord.
Don't be upset when others get rich
or when someone else's plans succeed.

MONTH 15
Psalm 40:3–5

³He put a new song in my mouth.
It was a song of praise to our God.
Many people will see this and worship him.
Then they will trust the Lord.
⁴Happy is the person
who trusts the Lord.
He doesn't turn to those who are proud,
to those who worship false gods.
⁵Lord our God, you have done many miracles.
Your plans for us are many.
If I tried to tell them all,
there would be too many to count.

MONTH 16
Psalm 41:1–3

¹Happy is the person who thinks about the poor.
When trouble comes, the Lord will save him.
²The Lord will protect him and spare his life.
The Lord will bless him in the land.
The Lord will not let his enemies take him.
³The Lord will give him strength when he is sick.
The Lord will make him well again.

MONTH 17
Psalm 46:1–3

¹God is our protection and our strength.
He always helps in times of trouble.
²So we will not be afraid if the earth shakes,
or if the mountains fall into the sea.
³We will not fear even if the oceans roar and foam,
or if the mountains shake at the raging sea.

MONTH 18
Psalm 46:8–11

⁸Come and see what the Lord has done.
He has done amazing things on the earth.
⁹He stops wars everywhere on the earth.
He breaks all bows and spears
and burns up the chariots with fire.
¹⁰God says, "Be still and know that I am God.
I will be praised in all the nations.
I will be praised throughout the earth."
¹¹The Lord of heaven's armies is with us.
The God of Jacob is our protection.

MONTH 19

Psalm 100:1–5

[1]Shout to the Lord, all the earth.
[2]Serve the Lord with joy.
Come before him with singing.
[3]Know that the Lord is God.
He made us, and we belong to him.
We are his people, the sheep he tends.
[4]Come into his city with songs of thanksgiving.
Come into his courtyards with songs of praise.
Thank him, and praise his name.
[5]The Lord is good. His love continues forever.
His loyalty continues from now on.

MONTH 20

Psalm 103:1–3

[1]All that I am, praise the Lord.
Everything in me, praise his holy name.
[2]My whole being, praise the Lord.
Do not forget all his kindnesses.
[3]The Lord forgives me for all my sins.
He heals all my diseases.

MONTH 21
Psalm 121:1–8

[1]I look up to the hills.
But where does my help come from?
[2]My help comes from the Lord.
He made heaven and earth.
[3]He will not let you be defeated.
He who guards you never sleeps.
[4]He who guards Israel
never rests or sleeps.
[5]The Lord guards you.
The Lord protects you as the shade protects you from the sun.
[6]The sun cannot hurt you during the day.
And the moon cannot hurt you at night.
[7]The Lord will guard you from all dangers.
He will guard your life.
[8]The Lord will guard you as you come and go,
both now and forever.

MONTH 22
Psalm 65:9–11
⁹You take care of the land and water it.
You make it very fertile.
The rivers of God are full of water.
Grain grows because you make it grow.
¹⁰You cause rain to fall on the plowed fields.
You soak them with water.
You soften the ground with rain.
And then you bless it.
¹¹You give the year a good harvest.
You load the wagons with many crops.

MONTH 23
Psalm 66:1–4
¹Everything on earth, shout with joy to God!
²Sing about his glory!
Make his praise glorious!
³Say to God, "Your works are amazing!
Your power is great.
Your enemies fall before you.
⁴All the earth worships you.
They sing praises to you.
They sing praises to your name."

MONTH 24
Psalm 119:9–11

[9]How can a young person live a pure life?
He can do it by obeying your word.
[10]With all my heart I try to obey you, God.
Don't let me break your commands.
[11]I have taken your words to heart
so I would not sin against you.

MONTH 25
Psalm 1:1–3

[1]Happy is the person who doesn't listen to the wicked.
He doesn't go where sinners go.
He doesn't do what bad people do.
[2]He loves the Lord's teachings.
He thinks about those teachings day and night.
[3]He is strong, like a tree planted by a river.
It produces fruit in season.
Its leaves don't die.
Everything he does will succeed.

MONTH 26
Psalm 18:16–19
[16]The Lord reached down from above and took me.
He pulled me from the deep water.
[17]He saved me from my powerful enemies.
Those who hated me were too strong for me.
[18]They attacked me at my time of trouble.
But the Lord supported me.
[19]He took me to a safe place.
Because he delights in me, he saved me.

MONTH 27
Psalm 18:33–36
[33]He makes me like a deer, which does not stumble.
He helps me stand on the steep mountains.
[34]He trains my hands for battle.
So my arms can bend a bronze bow.
[35]You protect me with your saving shield.
You support me with your right hand.
You have stooped to make me great.
[36]You give me a wide path on which to walk.
My feet have not slipped.

MONTH 28
Psalm 28:6–9

⁶Praise the Lord.
He heard my prayer for help.
⁷The Lord is my strength and shield.
I trust him, and he helps me.
I am very happy.
And I praise him with my song.
⁸The Lord is powerful.
He gives power and victory to his chosen one.
⁹Save your people.
Bless those who are your own.
Be their shepherd and carry them forever.

MONTH 29
Psalm 32:7–9

⁷You are my hiding place.
You protect me from my troubles.
You fill me with songs of salvation. Selah
⁸The Lord says, "I will make you wise.
I will show you where to go.
I will guide you and watch over you.
⁹So don't be like a horse or donkey.
They don't understand.
They must be led with bits and reins,
or they will not come near you."

MONTH 30
Psalm 34:17–19
[17]The Lord hears good people when they cry out to him.
He saves them from all their troubles.
[18]The Lord is close to the brokenhearted.
He saves those whose spirits have been crushed.
[19]People who do what is right may have many problems.
But the Lord will solve them all.

MONTH 31
Psalm 51:1–3
[1]God, be merciful to me
because you are loving.
Because you are always ready to be merciful,
wipe out all my wrongs.
[2]Wash away all my guilt
and make me clean again.
[3]I know about my wrongs.
I can't forget my sin.

MONTH 32
Psalm 62:5–8
[5]I wait patiently for God to save me.
Only he gives me hope.
[6]He is my rock, who saves me.
He protects me like a strong, walled city.
I will not be defeated.
[7]My honor and salvation come from God.
He is my mighty rock and my protection.
[8]People, trust God all the time.
Tell him all your problems.
God is our protection.

MONTH 33
Psalm 91:9–12
[9]The Lord is your protection.
You have made God Most High your place of safety.
[10]Nothing bad will happen to you.
No disaster will come to your home.
[11]He has put his angels in charge of you.
They will watch over you wherever you go.
[12]They will catch you with their hands.
And you will not hit your foot on a rock.

MONTH 34
Psalm 127:1–3
[1]If the Lord doesn't build the house,
the builders are working for nothing.
If the Lord doesn't guard the city,
the guards are watching for nothing.
[2]It is no use for you to get up early
and stay up late,
working for a living.
The Lord gives sleep to those he loves.
[3]Children are a gift from the Lord.
Babies are a reward.

MONTH 35
Psalm 139:1–4
[1]Lord, you have examined me.
You know all about me.
[2]You know when I sit down and when I get up.
You know my thoughts before I think them.
[3]You know where I go and where I lie down.
You know well everything I do.
[4]Lord, even before I say a word,
you already know what I am going to say.

MONTH 36
Psalm 139:13–18

[13]You made my whole being.
You formed me in my mother's body.
[14]I praise you because you made me in
an amazing and wonderful way.
What you have done is wonderful.
I know this very well.
[15]You saw my bones being formed
as I took shape in my mother's body.
When I was put together there,
[16]you saw my body as it was formed.
All the days planned for me
were written in your book
before I was one day old.
[17]God, your thoughts are precious to me.
They are so many!
[18]If I could count them,
they would be more than all the grains of sand.
When I wake up,
I am still with you.

ACKNOWLEDGMENTS

I cannot express enough thanks to the Holy God, the author of knowledge and wisdom for having given me this opportunity and sustained me during the entire process of completing this book.

I gratefully appreciate and acknowledge the various pastors and church groups who allowed me to speak and teach on the concepts of this book.

To all my relatives, and friends who shared their support and encouragement, thank you!

NOTES

Chapter 1

1 Josh McDowell and David H. Bellis, *The Last Christian Generation* (Holiday, Florida: Green Key Books, 2006), page 13.

2 Billy Graham, *How to Be Born Again* (W Publishing Group/Thomas Nelson, Nashville, TN 1989), page 8.

3 Max Lucado, *When God Whispers Your Name* (Nashville: Thomas Nelson, 2009), page 10.

4 Albert Williams, *Wasted Years* (1960).

5 Augustine of Hippo "public domain."

6 Graham, *How to Be Born Again*, (W Publishing Group/Thomas Nelson, Nashville, TN 1989), page 64.

7 Charles B. Templeton, *Farewell to God* (McClelland & Stewart, Toronto, Ontario 1996).

8 The Gideons International, *New Testament, Psalms and Proverbs* (Nashville, TN 1960).

9 John F. DeVries, *Why Pray?* (Mission India, Grand Rapids, MI 2014), page 253

10 Wikipedia, [https://en.wikipedia.org/wiki/Hunger_strike].

Chapter 2

11 Barbara J. Sahakian and Jamie Nicole LaBuzetta, *Bad Moves: How Decision-Making Goes Wrong, and the Ethics of Smart Drugs* (Oxford, UK: Oxford University Press, 2013), page 21.

12 Brian Wansink and Jeffery Sobal, "Mindless Eating: The 200 Daily Food Decisions We Overlook," *Environment and Behavior* (Los Angeles: SAGE Publishing, 2007), pages 39, 106–123.

13 Michael Rydelnik and Michael Vanlaningham, *The Moody Bible Commentary* (Moody Publishers, Chicago IL 2014), page 1949.

14 Warren Wiersbe, *Life Sentences* (Grand Rapids, Michigan: Zondervan Publishing, 2007), page 43.

Chapter 3

15 *The Merriam-Webster Dictionary*, definitions of *challenge* and *suffering* (Merriam-Webster Incorporated, Springfield, Massachusetts 2015)

16 Brent Curtis and John Eldredge, *Sacred Romance* [Thomas Nelson, Nashville, TN 1997), page 25.

17 Biography of Blaise Pascal, Wikipedia [https://en.wikipedia.org/wiki/Blaise_Pascal].

18 Ravi Zacharias, *Jesus among Other Gods* [W Publishing Group,Nashville,TN 2000] page 123.

19 Rydelnik and Vanlaningham, *The Moody Bible Commentary*, (Moody Publishers, Chicago IL 2014) page 1470.

20 Francis Chan, *Crazy Love*, (David C Cook,Colorado Springs,CO 2008) page 40.

21 Mary Stevenson, "Footprints in the Sand" …. [public domain].

22 Joseph Scheumann, *Five Truths about Christian Suffering* (https://www.desiringgod.org/articles/five-truths-about-christian-suffering)

23 Rydelnik and Vanlaningham, *The Moody Bible Commentary*, (Moody Publishers, Chicago IL 2014) page 1559.

24 Rydelnik and Vanlaningham, *The Moody Bible Commentary*, (Moody Publishers, Chicago IL 2014) page 1841.

25 Wikipedia, definition of *Spiritual Warefare* [https://en.wikipedia.org/wiki/Spiritual_warfare]

26 John Bevere, *The Bait of Satan*,(Charisma House, Lake Mary, Florida 2013)

27 Chuck D. Pierce, *The Spiritual Warfare Handbook* (Chosen, Minneapolis, Minnesota 2000)

28 Wikipedia, definition of *talisman*, [https://en.wikipedia.org/wiki/Talismanin]

29 Derek Prince, *Spiritual Warfare*…. [Derek Prince Ministries, Trichy, Tamilnadu, India 1987).

30 Prince, *Spiritual Warfare*… [Derek Prince Ministries, Trichy, Tamilnadu, India 1987].

31 Prince, *Spiritual Warfare*… [Derek Prince Ministries, Trichy, Tamilnadu, India 1987].

32 Michael Ramsden, *Has Christianity failed you?* [Fox Theatre, Atlanta, GA 2006]

33 Derek Prince, *Spiritual Warfare,* ... [Derek Prince Ministries, Trichy, Tamilnadu,India 1987].

34 Joseph Bergeron, MD, *The Crucifixion of Jesus: A Medical Doctor Examines the Death and Resurrection of Christ,* [St. Polycarp Publishing House,Cumming,GA 2018] page 59

35 Derek Prince, *God's Atomic Weapon: The Blood of Jesus,* [https://www.youtube.com/watch?v=R4U_1oRX7_Q&t].

36 *The Merriam-Webster Dictionary,* definition of *yoga,*[https://www.merriam-webster.com/dictionary].

37 John Calvin; Henry Beveridge, Translator, *The Institutes of the Christian Religion* (Grand Rapids, Michigan: Christian Classics Ethereal Library, 2002; public domain), https://www.ccel.org/ccel/calvin/institutes.iii.xv.html, Chapter 14, section 6.

38 Billy Graham, *Angels* (Thomas Nelson, Nashville, TN 1995), page xvii.

39 Dietrich Bonhoeffer, *The Cost of Discipleship* (Touchstone, New York,NY 1995), page 57.

Chapter 4

40 Rydelnik and Vanlaningham, *Moody Bible Commentary,* (Moody Publishers, Chicago IL 2014) page 1802.

41 Don Fleming, *Daniel,* Concise Bible Commentary (AMG Publishers, Chattanooga, TN 2002).

42 Rydelnik and Vanlaningham, *The Moody Bible Commentary,* (Moody Publishers, Chicago IL 2014) page 917.

43 William Carey[https://www.azquotes.com/author/2464-William_Carey].

44 Ravi Zacharias, The Grand Weaver (Zondervan, Grand Rapids, MI 2007), 39–40.

Chapter 5

45 Dallas Willard, *Renovation of the Heart* (Navpress, Colorado Springs, CO,2002), page 14.

46 Rydelnik and Vanlaningham, *Moody Bible Commentary,* (Moody Publishers, Chicago IL 2014) page 1840.

47 *The Merriam-Webster Dictionary*, [https://www.merriam-webster.com/dictionary/credibility] `.

48 James M. Kouzes and Barry Z. Poser, *Credibility: How Leaders Gain and Lose It, Why People Demand It* (City, State: Jossey-Bass, 2011), page 25.

49 Rydelnik and Vanlaningham, *The Moody Bible Commentary*, (Moody Publishers, Chicago IL 2014) page 1839.

50 Henry Cloud and John Townsend, *Boundaries: When to Say Yes, How to Say No to Take Control of Your Life* (Zondervan, Grand Rapids, Michigan: 2017).

51 Justin Taylor, "5 Quotes from G. K. Chesterton on Gratitude and Thanksgiving," The Gospel Coalition blog, November 27, 2014.

52 Mental Toughness Inc., *Definition of mental toughness* [https://www.mentaltoughnessinc.com/].

53 Henry Wadsworth Longfellow, "The Ladder of St. Augustine," poetryfoundation.org.

Chapter 6

54 Jack Kelly, *More Than Half of U.S. Workers Are Unhappy In Their Jobs: Here's Why And What Needs To Be Done Now* "[https://www.forbes.com/sites/jackkelly/2019/10/25/more-than-half-of-us-workers-are-unhappy-in-their-jobs-heres-why-and-what-needs-to-be-done-now/?sh=4fc6295e2024"], October 25, 2019.

55 Staff Squared HR, *Why 85% of People Hate their Jobs*, [https://www.staffsquared.com/blog/why-85-of-people-hate-their-jobs/], December 3, 2020].

56 Warren Wiersbe, *So That's What a Christian Is!* (Baker Book House Company,Grand Rapids, MI 1996) page 131.

57 John C. Maxwell, Stephen R. Graves and Thomas G. Addington, *Life @ Work, Marketplace Success for People of Faith* (Thomas Nelson,Nashville,TN 2005), page 28.

58 *The Merriam-Webster Dictionary*, definition of *career*, [https://www.merriam-webster.com/dictionary/career].

59 Maxwell, Graves and Addington, *Life @ Work, Marketplace Success for People of Faith*, (Thomas Nelson, Nashville,TN 2005) page 74.

60 Os Guinness, *The Call* (W Publishing Group/Thomas Nelson, Nashville, TN 1998), page 4.

61 Rydelnik and Vanlaningham, *The Moody Bible Commentary*, (Moody Publishers, Chicago IL 2014) page 422

62 Wikipedia, Dr. Ida Sophia Scudder, https://en.wikipedia.org/wiki/Ida_S._Scudder.

Chapter 7

63 Moody Bible Institute, *Today in the Word* (Moody Publishers, Chicago IL October 2020) page 23.

64 Moody Bible Institute, *Today in the Word*, (Moody Publishers, Chicago IL October 2020) page 23.

65 Lt. Carey H. Cash, *A Table in the Presence* (W Publishing Group/Thomas Nelson, Nashville, TN 2004).

CPSIA information can be obtained
at www.ICGtesting.com
Printed in the USA
LVHW111513250322
714397LV00006B/156